STRESS-FREE MOORING

FOR SAIL & POWER

DUNCAN WELLS

ADLARD COLES

LONDON · OXFORD · NEW YORK · NEW DELHI · SYDNEY

ADLARD COLES
Bloomsbury Publishing Plc
50 Bedford Square, London, WC1B 3DP, UK

BLOOMSBURY, ADLARD COLES and the Adlard Coles logo are trademarks of
Bloomsbury Publishing Plc

First published in Great Britain 2020

A catalogue record for this book is available from the British Library

Library of Congress Cataloguing-in-Publication data has been applied for

ISBN: PB: 978-1-4729-6835-7; ePDF: 978-1-4729-6833-3; eBook: 978-1-4729-6834-0

10 9 8 7 6 5 4 3 2 1

Designed and typeset in Bliss Light by Susan McIntyre
Printed and bound in India by Replika Press Pvt. Ltd.

To find out more about our authors and books visit www.bloomsbury.com and sign up for our newsletters

Contents

Contents

This book presents a bite-sized version of *Stress-Free Sailing* and *Stress-Free Motorboating* with pictorial diagrams to allow you to compare the conditions you are experiencing with a range of options and choose the appropriate technique to help you moor your boat in a stress-free manner.

When it comes to casting off, consider:

- how you are moored (finger berth or alongside)
- how your boat behaves under engine
- how your boat is affected by the wind (windage)
- the conditions (wind and tide) you are experiencing

and locate the relevant page in the book, to see the techniques for getting off.

For coming alongside, check the berth and conditions and select a technique for getting on. Plan this well in advance of arriving at the dock.

Also included are handy hints, and some of the best advice I can offer. And the very best advice is: don't fight it. Work with it. Use the conditions to your advantage.

If you are being pinned on by wind and tide to a stretch of pontoon, it might be best just to put the kettle on and wait until conditions are favourable for a departure.

If you are arriving at an unfamiliar port, try to choose a favourable berth, into the tide, and be aware of the effect of a wind blowing you on and one that is blowing you away from the dock and what you need to do to counter the effect. Try to keep upwind to buy yourself some space.

On sailing boats, all the techniques I recommend can be managed by one person from the cockpit of the boat. Some techniques can be managed by one person on a motorboat, while others will require a skipper and a crewmember.

Wind direction is shown thus:

Wind strength is shown thus:

    for winds of up to 20 knots

    for winds of less than 10 knots

Of course the power of the wind, and the effect it will have on your boat, differs greatly from when it is beam on – when you experience the full force of the wind pushing you on to, or off, the dock – to when it is on the bow or the stern and the effect is lessened.

Tide or current stream is shown thus:

KEY TO COLOUR CODE

| Sail |
| Power |
| Sail & Power |

Preface

OXO – SECURING A LINE TO A CLEAT

1. Lead the line around the cleat.
2. Make a complete turn: O.
3. Cross over once and then again: X.
4. Complete another turn: O.

O

Plus a locking hitch after the second 'O'...

X

Or the locking hitch after the 'X' and no second 'O'.

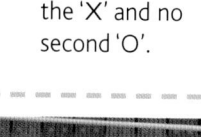

O

---

1. Lead the line around the cleat.
2. Make a complete turn: O.
3. Cross over once and then again: X.
4. Complete another turn: O.

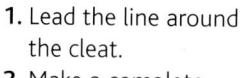 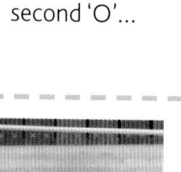     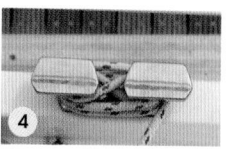

O

Plus a locking hitch after the second 'O'...

X

Or the locking hitch after the 'X' and no second 'O'.

O

SHARING A CLEAT

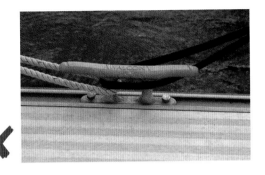

Sometimes you'll have to find space for your line on a busy cleat like this.

Tie a bowline in the end of your line, feed it under everyone else's and over the top of the cleat.

If your line is attached like this, others can easily release it to get theirs out.

Preparation

LASSOING

If you can lasso in the boating business, you're in business!

The keys to good lassoing:

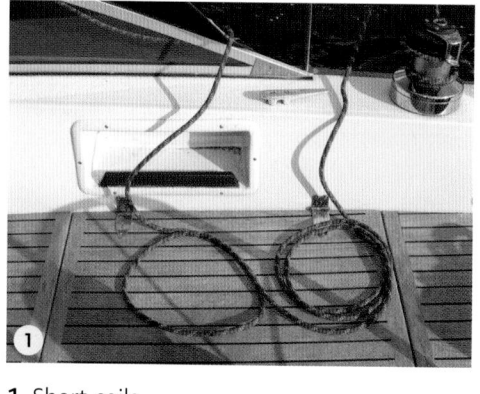

1. Short coils.

2. Throw high and wide.

3. Don't let go of the running end.

COILING A ROPE

Finishing off...

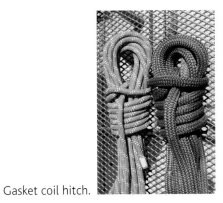

Gasket coil hitch.

Sailor's way.

Navy way.

Preparation

FENDER UP WELL

Down to the water and up a bit for pontoon height.

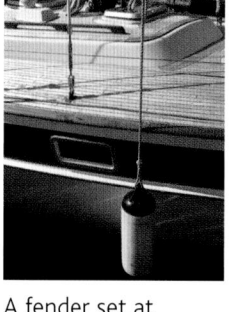

A fender set at pontoon height...

Becomes a fender set at gunwale height for rafting up or to protect against a neighbour...

When taken under the lower guard wire and over the upper guard wire.

When taken under the lower guard wire and over the upper guard wire...

Becomes, in an instant, a fender set at gunwale height.

HOW TO SET YOUR MOORING LINES (WARPS)

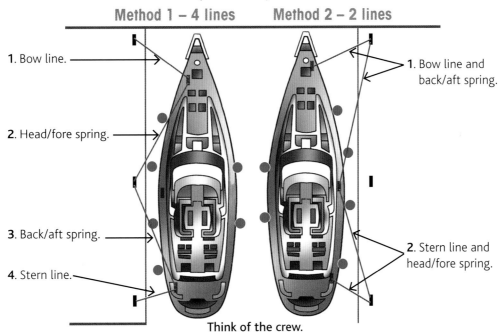

Method 1 – 4 lines   Method 2 – 2 lines

1. Bow line.

2. Head/fore spring.

3. Back/aft spring.

4. Stern line.

1. Bow line and back/aft spring.

2. Stern line and head/fore spring.

Think of the crew.
Using 4 lines (one line, one job) cut to length will mean lines are
shorter and easier to manage than using 2 long lines to do the 4 jobs.

Preparation

HOW TO SET YOUR MOORING LINES (WARPS)

Method 1 – 4 lines (one line one job)

Method 2 – 2 lines

1. Bow line.
2. Head spring from bow to shore cleat amidships.
3. Back spring from stern to shore cleat amidships.
4. Stern line.

1. Bow to shore cleat to midship cleat as a back spring.
2. Stern to shore cleat to midship cleat as a head spring.

Springs set from bow and stern to a shore cleat amidships will prevent yawing and will help to hold the boat in, so that it lies alongside nicely.

HOW TO SET YOUR MOORING LINES (WARPS)

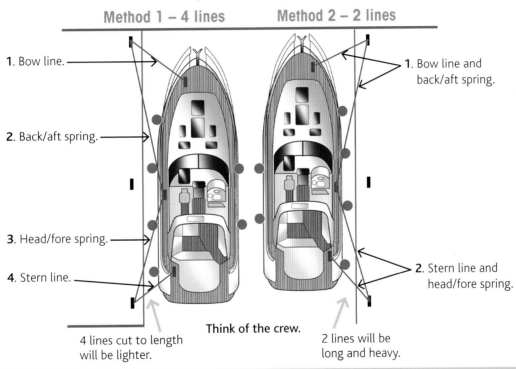

Method 1 – 4 lines

Method 2 – 2 lines

1. Bow line.

2. Back/aft spring.

3. Head/fore spring.

4. Stern line.

1. Bow line and back/aft spring.

2. Stern line and head/fore spring.

Think of the crew.

4 lines cut to length will be lighter.

2 lines will be long and heavy.

Preparation

HOW TO SET YOUR MOORING LINES (WARPS)

Method 1 – 4 lines (one line one job)

1. Bow line.
2. Back spring taken shore to midship cleat.
3. Head spring taken shore to midship cleat.
4. Stern line.

Being flat sided, motorboats tend not to yaw about on their mooring and so setting springs to a midship cleat on board is fine.

Method 2 – 2 lines

1. Bow to shore cleat to midship cleat as a back spring.
2. Stern to shore cleat to midship cleat as a head spring.

PARTS OF THE BOAT AND THE TERMS USED

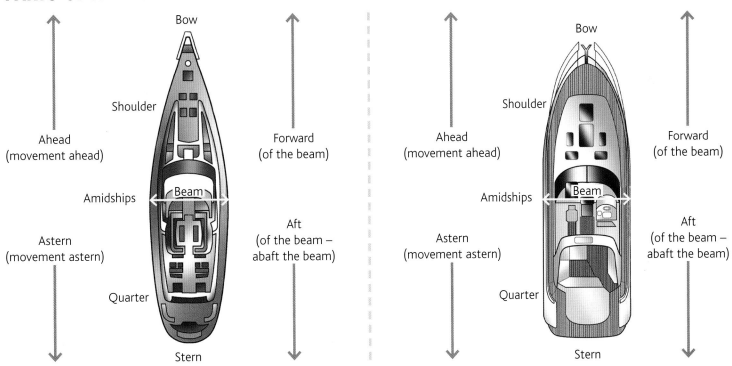

Bow

Shoulder

Ahead
(movement ahead)

Forward
(of the beam)

Amidships

Beam

Astern
(movement astern)

Aft
(of the beam –
abaft the beam)

Quarter

Stern

Bow

Shoulder

Ahead
(movement ahead)

Forward
(of the beam)

Amidships

Beam

Astern
(movement astern)

Aft
(of the beam –
abaft the beam)

Quarter

Stern

Preparation

WIND DIRECTION AND SPEED

- **Wind direction** refers to where the wind is coming from.
- A north wind is coming from the north.

- **Initial wind** – wind direction stated in the forecast.
- **Backing** – wind direction moves anticlockwise, from N to NW.
- **Veering** – wind direction moves clockwise, from N to NE.

Backed   Initial   Veered

- **Wind speed** is measured in knots and **wind force** according to the Beaufort scale.

- When wind blows over the surface of the Earth, friction causes it to slow and to back by 15° over the sea and by 30° over the land.

Wind shear
Wind strength at the top of the mast will be greater than wind strength on deck – wind reduces in speed as it meets more resistance. It also backs.

MEASURING THE SPEED OF THE TIDE BY EYE

1. Drop a scrunched-up piece of kitchen towel*
in at the bow.

2. Time how long it takes to reach the stern.

3. Use this equation to calculate the speed
of the tide.

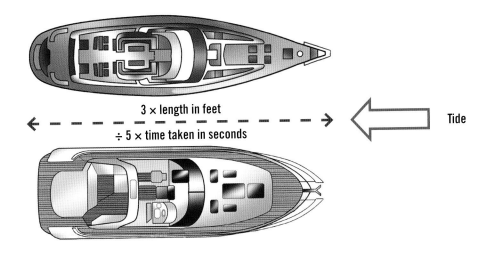

3 × length in feet

÷ 5 × time taken in seconds

Tide

Example:
Boat length 35',
Time taken 14",
so $\dfrac{3 \times 35}{5 \times 14}$

$= \dfrac{105}{70}$

= 1.5 knots tide

*Kitchen towel will sink and dissolve and if scrunched up it takes longer to disappear out of sight in the water. Bread rolls or anything that floats will be measuring the wind effect as much as the tide – you want the speed of the tide only. You could use twigs and leaves as they float by.

Preparation

WIND AND TIDE OPPOSED – WHICH HAS THE GREATER EFFECT ON THE BOAT?

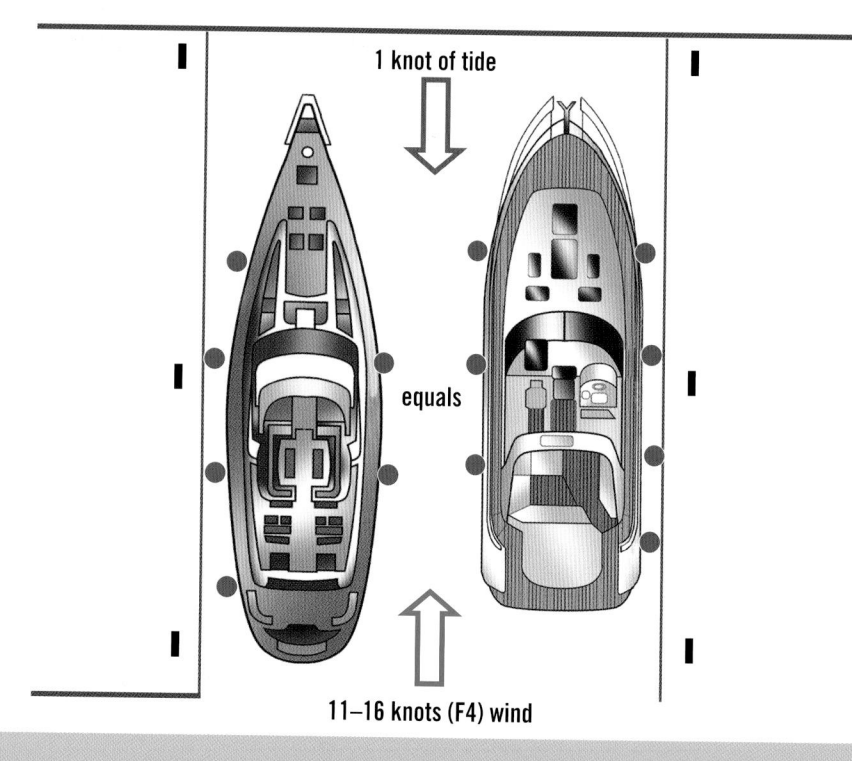

1 knot of tide

equals

11–16 knots (F4) wind

BOATS STEER FROM THE STERN

In a car, when you turn the wheel to the right, the front wheels take the car to the right. In a boat, when you turn the helm to the right (tiller to the left) to turn the boat to starboard, it is not the bow that moves to the right but the stern that moves to the left, and this makes the bow move to the right.

So if you are about to hit something on your port side, the last thing you need to do is to turn to starboard because this will send your stern to port and straight into what you were trying to avoid. It is counter-intuitive, but to avoid something on port you need to turn to port to throw your stern away from it. You then need to stop and back out of the situation.

Boats pivot from a point about a third of the way from the bow when going ahead, and from a point about a third of the way from the stern when going astern.

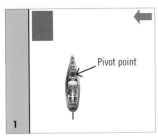

Wind pushing you towards the obstruction.

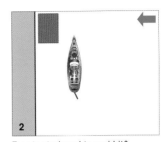

Turn to starboard to avoid it?

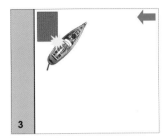

Perhaps not...

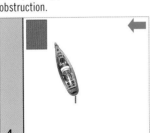

Turn to port to avoid it.

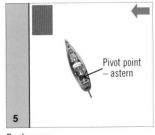

Back away...

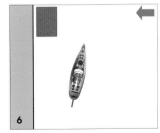

Allowing for the effect of the wind, drive ahead.

Preparation

BOATS STEER FROM THE STERN

In a car, when you turn the wheel to the right, the front wheels take the car to the right. In a boat, when you turn the helm to the right (tiller to the left) to turn the boat to starboard, it is not the bow that moves to the right but the stern that moves to the left, and this makes the bow move to the right.

So if you are about to hit something on your port side, the last thing you need to do is to turn to starboard because this will send your stern to port and straight into what you were trying to avoid. It is counter-intuitive, but to avoid something on port you need to turn to port to throw your stern away from it. You then need to stop and back out of the situation.

Boats pivot from a point about a third of the way from the bow when going ahead, and from a point about a third of the way from the stern when going astern.

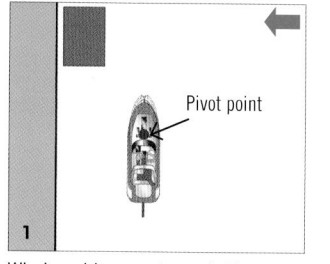

1

Wind pushing you towards the obstruction.

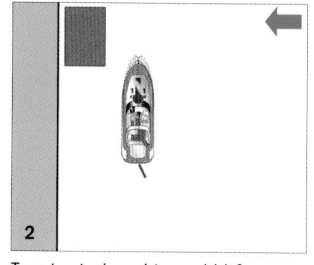

2

Turn to starboard to avoid it?

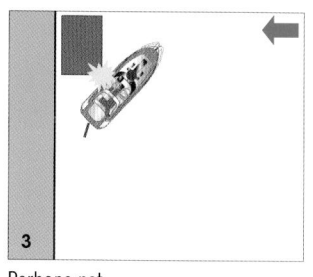

3

Perhaps not...

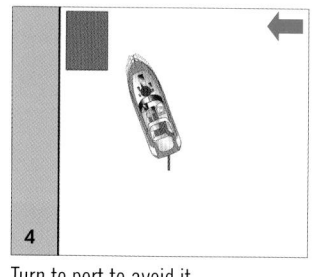

4

Turn to port to avoid it.

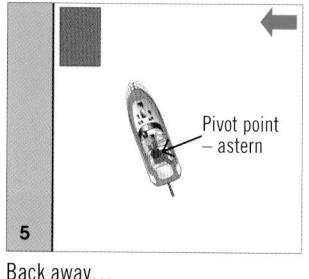

5

Back away...

6

Allowing for the effect of the wind, drive ahead.

WHICH WAY DO YOU KICK ASTERN – SINGLE ENGINE?

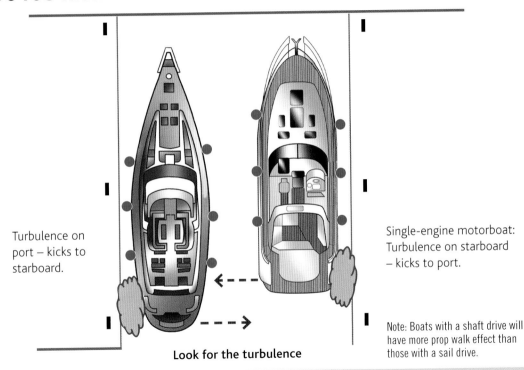

Turbulence on port – kicks to starboard.

Single-engine motorboat: Turbulence on starboard – kicks to port.

Note: Boats with a shaft drive will have more prop walk effect than those with a sail drive.

Look for the turbulence

Preparation

READY RECKONER – STARBOARD PROP WALK ASTERN
Single-engine boat – what the bow and stern will do

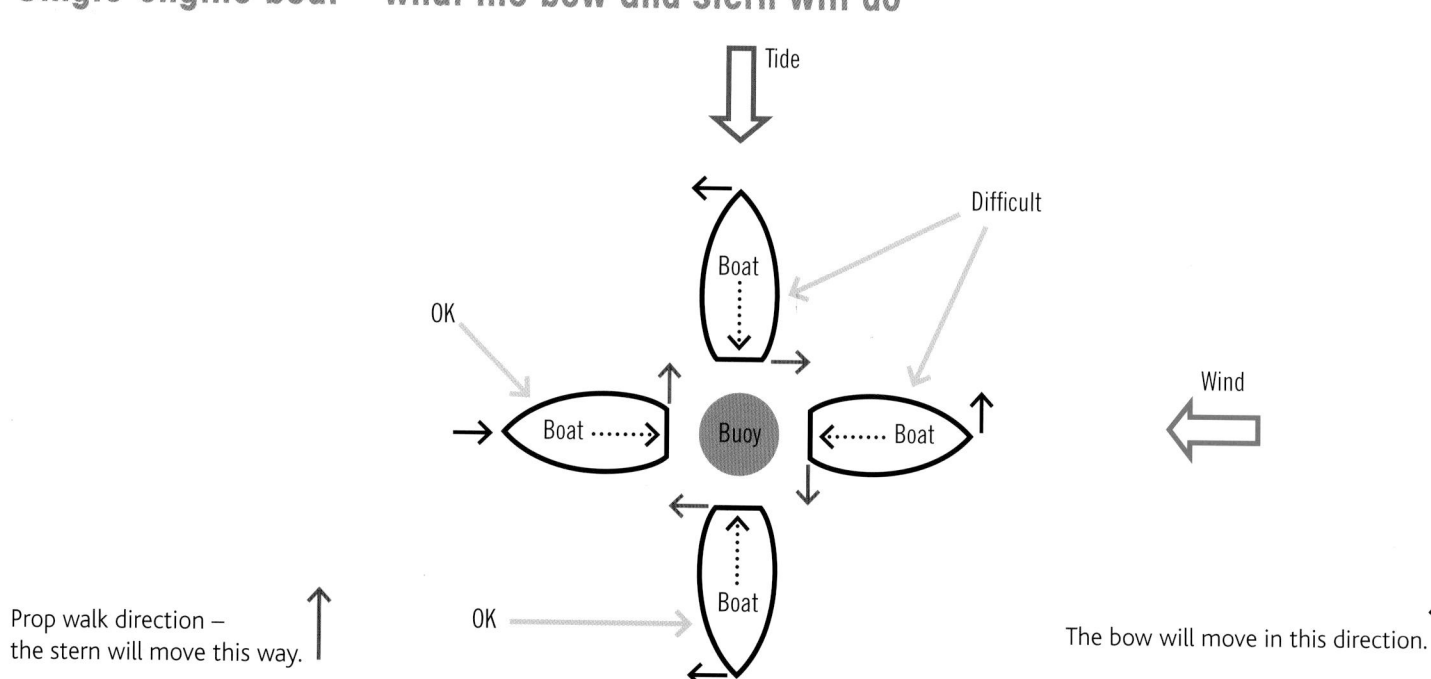

Prop walk direction –
the stern will move this way.

OK

The bow will move in this direction.

USING PROP WALK ON A TWIN-ENGINE BOAT

Bows to

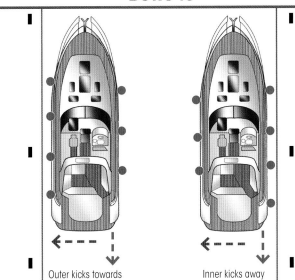

Outer kicks towards

Inner kicks away

1. By convention, the outer engine in astern kicks the boat into the dock.

2. The inner engine in astern kicks the boat away from the dock.

Stern to

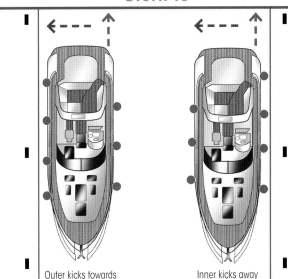

Outer kicks towards

Inner kicks away

1. By convention, the outer engine in astern kicks the boat into the dock.

2. The inner engine in astern kicks the boat away from the dock.

Preparation

TWIN-RUDDER BOATS – NO THRUSTERS

   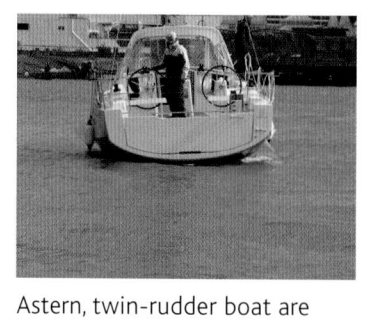

Manoeuvrability on single-engine boats comes from a flow of water over the rudder, either through speed through the water or from the propeller.

As the propeller on a twin-rudder boat does not throw much of any water over the rudders, you need more speed through the water...

to handle close-quarter manoeuvres. Using prop walk astern will also help to make turns tighter. Thrusters will help too, of course.

Astern, twin-rudder boat are generally responsive as long as you have a good flow of water over the rudders.

GET A GRIP! (On the water)

2 knots of boat speed against
1 knot of tide/current
= 1 knot over the ground

2 knots of boat speed
+ 1 knot of tide/current
= 3 knots over the ground
= too fast with no means of stopping

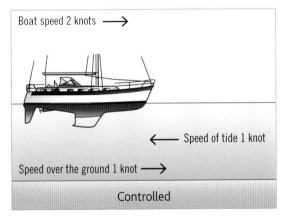

Boat speed 2 knots →

← Speed of tide 1 knot

Speed over the ground 1 knot →

Controlled

Happiness!

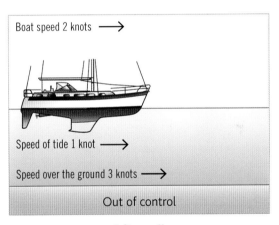

Boat speed 2 knots →

Speed of tide 1 knot →

Speed over the ground 3 knots →

Out of control

Misery!!

Preparation

GET A GRIP! (On the water)

2 knots of boat speed against
1 knot of tide/current
= 1 knot over the ground

  2 knots of boat speed
+ 1 knot of tide/current
= 3 knots over the ground
= too fast with no means of stopping

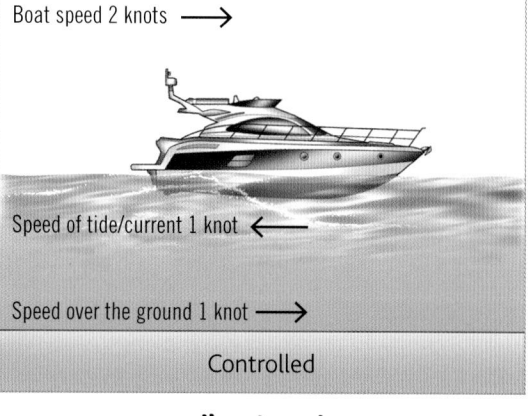

Boat speed 2 knots →

Speed of tide/current 1 knot ←

Speed over the ground 1 knot →

Controlled

Happiness!

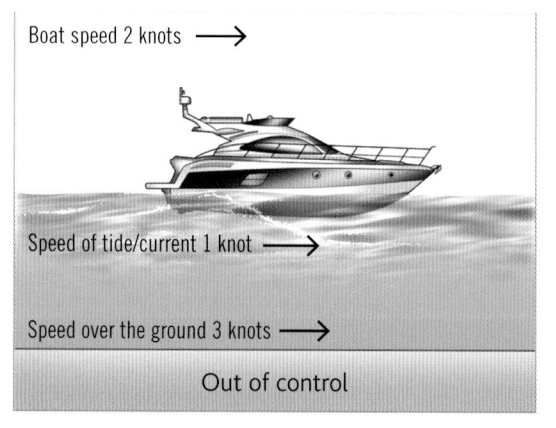

Boat speed 2 knots →

Speed of tide/current 1 knot →

Speed over the ground 3 knots →

Out of control

Misery!!

TYING THE RUSTLER'S HITCH – tied from seaward, so you can release it from onboard

1. Take a bight under what you wish to attach to – here, the cleat.

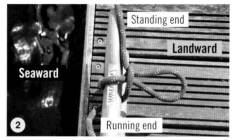

2. Take a bight of the standing end through this bight – tighten on the running end.

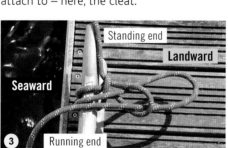

3. Take a bight of the running end through this bight and...

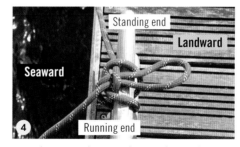

4. Tighten on the standing end. To release, give the running end a sharp tug.

Preparation

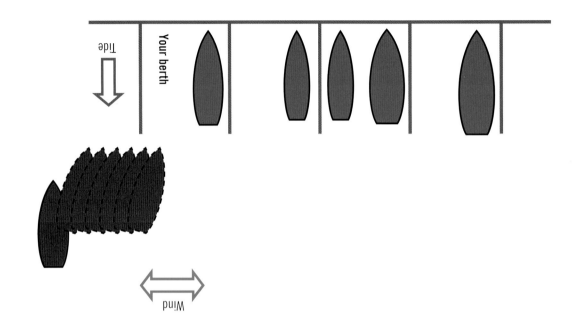

Tide

Your berth

Wind

FERRY GLIDING

Ferry gliding from the middle of the river to the bank – the barge is angled just slightly across the current and clicked into ahead to motor against the current without any forward movement over the ground, so she goes sideways.

The sailing boat has left her berth and is motoring ahead against the tide at a slight angle so she goes sideways without going forwards and makes her way out into the fairway.

Preparation

MAKING A TWIN-ENGINE BOAT GO SIDEWAYS

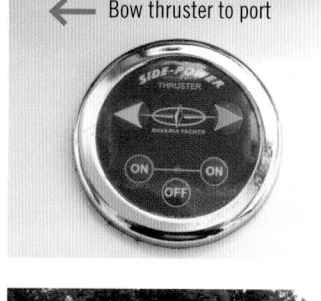

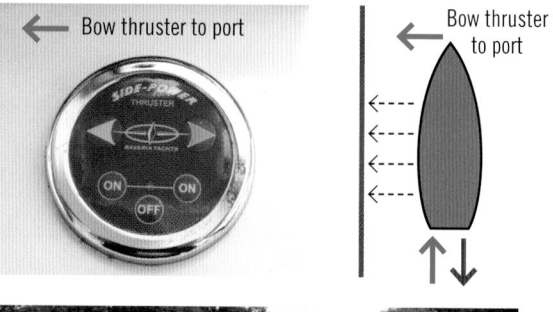

Bow thruster to port

Bow thruster to port

- Port engine ahead.
- Starboard engine astern.
- Bow thruster pushing bow to port.

The boat will go to port. Adjust the amount of engine revs required (clicked into gear is usually sufficient) and bow thruster required to go sideways without any movement ahead or astern.

Coming sideways on to the dock.

MAKING A SINGLE-ENGINE BOAT GO SIDEWAYS

Helm hard to port, engine clicked into ahead, pushes water off the rudder to move the stern to starboard. Bow thruster to starboard and bow goes to starboard. Balance the engine against the bow thruster to reduce movement ahead and go to starboard, sideways.

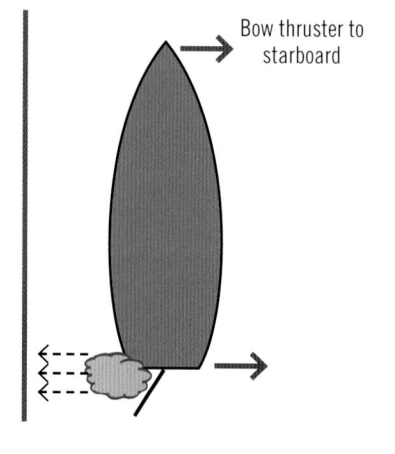

Bow thruster to starboard

ENGINE CHECKS

You are going to use engines to effect these manoeuvres and you need to know that they will not let you down at a crucial moment, so they need to be serviced regularly.

Daily engine checks:

W – Water: Fresh water, check the header tank. Check the raw water filter.*

O – Oil: Engine oil. Periodically check gear box oil as well.

B – Belt: Alternator belt, looks OK? Tension OK? Half an inch of play.

B – Battery: Topped up, terminals look OK?

L – Leaks: Any nasty leaks under the engine?

E – Exhaust: Water coming out of the exhaust when the engine is running?

A ping-pong ball in the raw water filter shows you immediately that the water is flowing through it.

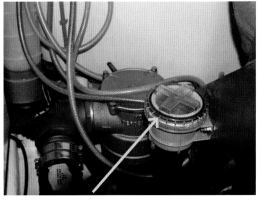

*Take care when replacing the raw water filter cap that the O-ring or seal is there and has not fallen out.

No seal
= air allowed in
= no flow
= engine overheating.

Preparation

YOUR BERTH – MAKE IT YOUR OWN

Stow a line on a perch...

Ready.

Motorboats and sailing boats don't make great neighbours.

Convenient post to stow a line.

With dock fenders, there is no need for boat fenders.

Stanchion in line with pile means boat is positioned correctly within the berth.

WHAT IF YOU HAVE NO MIDSHIP CLEAT?

A block on the genoa sheet lead track.

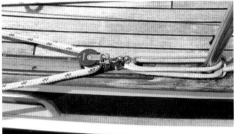

A snatch block at the base of a stanchion.

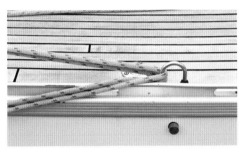

A 'D' ring amidships.

A snatch block clipped to the gunwale/toerail.

A snatch block on a carabiner around the base of the shrouds.

Using a stanchion as a midship cleat.

Preparation

HOW THE WIND AND TIDE WILL AFFECT YOU – BOWS IN – BLOWN OFF THE DOCK

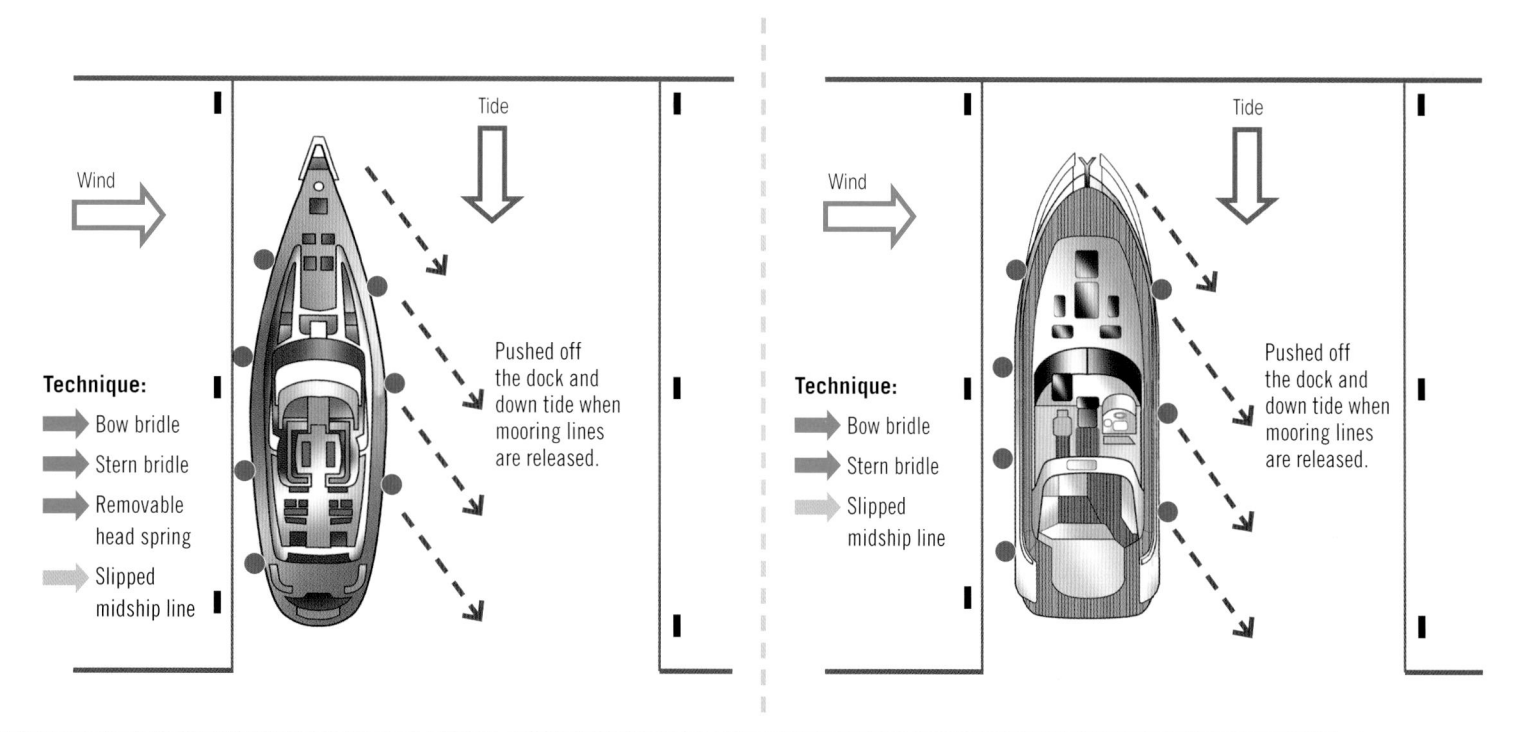

Technique:

➡ Bow bridle

➡ Stern bridle

➡ Removable head spring

➡ Slipped midship line

Wind

Tide

Pushed off the dock and down tide when mooring lines are released.

Technique:

➡ Bow bridle

➡ Stern bridle

➡ Slipped midship line

Wind

Tide

Pushed off the dock and down tide when mooring lines are released.

HOW THE WIND AND TIDE WILL AFFECT YOU – STERN IN – BLOWN OFF THE DOCK

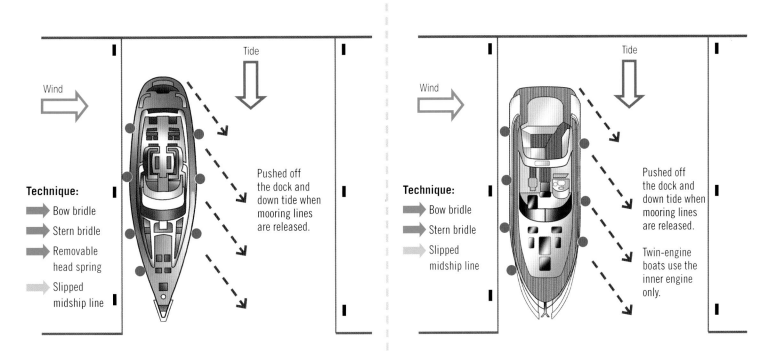

Tide

Wind

Technique:

➤ Bow bridle

➤ Stern bridle

➤ Removable head spring

➤ Slipped midship line

Pushed off the dock and down tide when mooring lines are released.

Tide

Wind

Technique:

➤ Bow bridle

➤ Stern bridle

➤ Slipped midship line

Pushed off the dock and down tide when mooring lines are released.

Twin-engine boats use the inner engine only.

Casting Off

HOW THE WIND AND TIDE WILL AFFECT YOU – BOWS IN – BLOWN ON TO THE DOCK

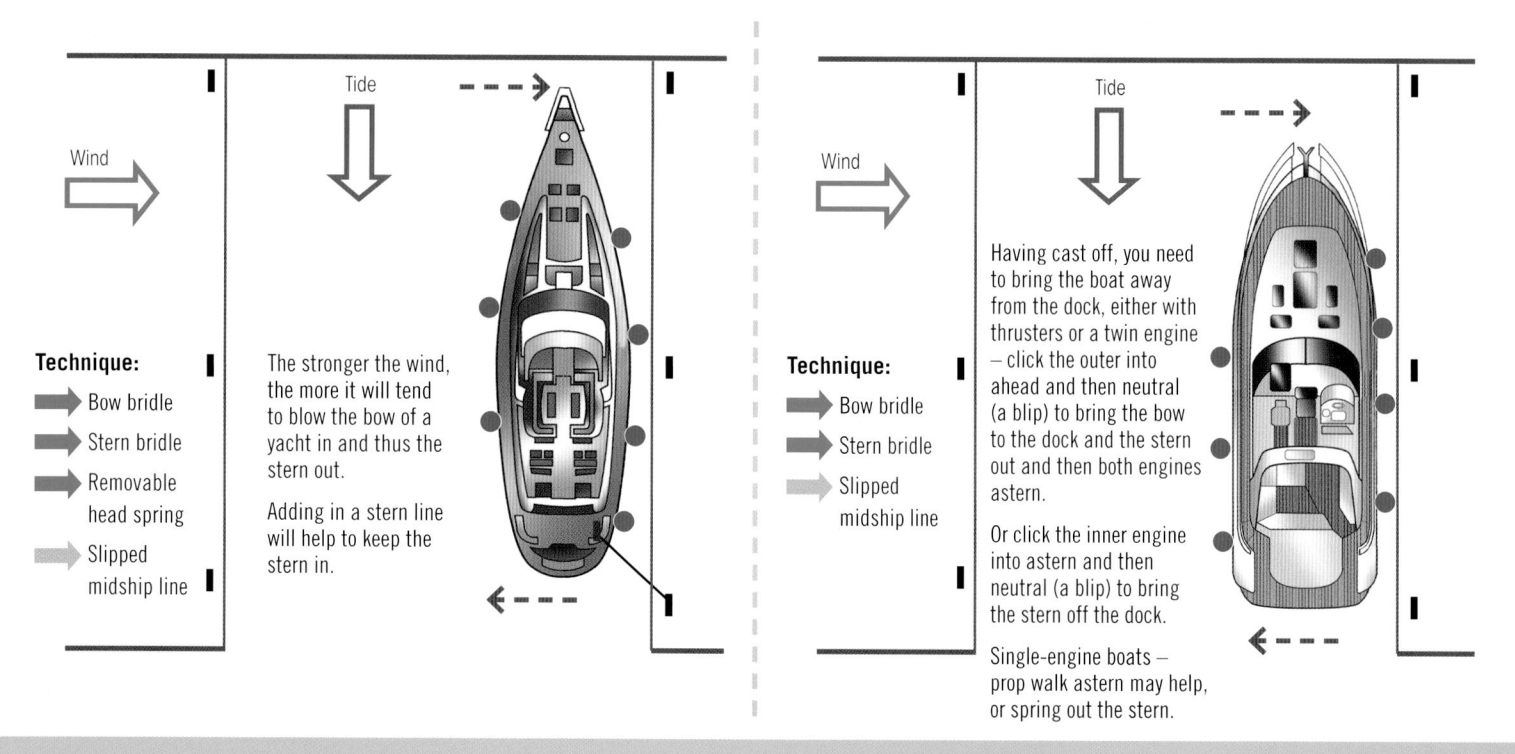

Wind

Tide

Technique:

➤ Bow bridle

➤ Stern bridle

➤ Removable head spring

➤ Slipped midship line

The stronger the wind, the more it will tend to blow the bow of a yacht in and thus the stern out.

Adding in a stern line will help to keep the stern in.

Wind

Tide

Technique:

➤ Bow bridle

➤ Stern bridle

➤ Slipped midship line

Having cast off, you need to bring the boat away from the dock, either with thrusters or a twin engine – click the outer into ahead and then neutral (a blip) to bring the bow to the dock and the stern out and then both engines astern.

Or click the inner engine into astern and then neutral (a blip) to bring the stern off the dock.

Single-engine boats – prop walk astern may help, or spring out the stern.

TIDE ON THE BOW

Bows to the tide will push you back from the finger and then in ahead you have grip on the water and are in control as you drive out into the fairway.

Fairway

Tide

If there is little or no tide, it could be the wind that is the dominant force.

TIDE ON THE STERN

With tide on the stern, you need plenty of room as you need to be going faster than the speed of the tide when in ahead to gain grip. So you need to buy yourself as much space as possible to make the turn into the fairway without hitting the end of the pontoon – or you could exit astern into the tide.

Tide

Fairway

If there is little or no tide, it could be the wind that is the dominant force.

Casting Off

SPRING, BRIDLE, SLIPPED LINES

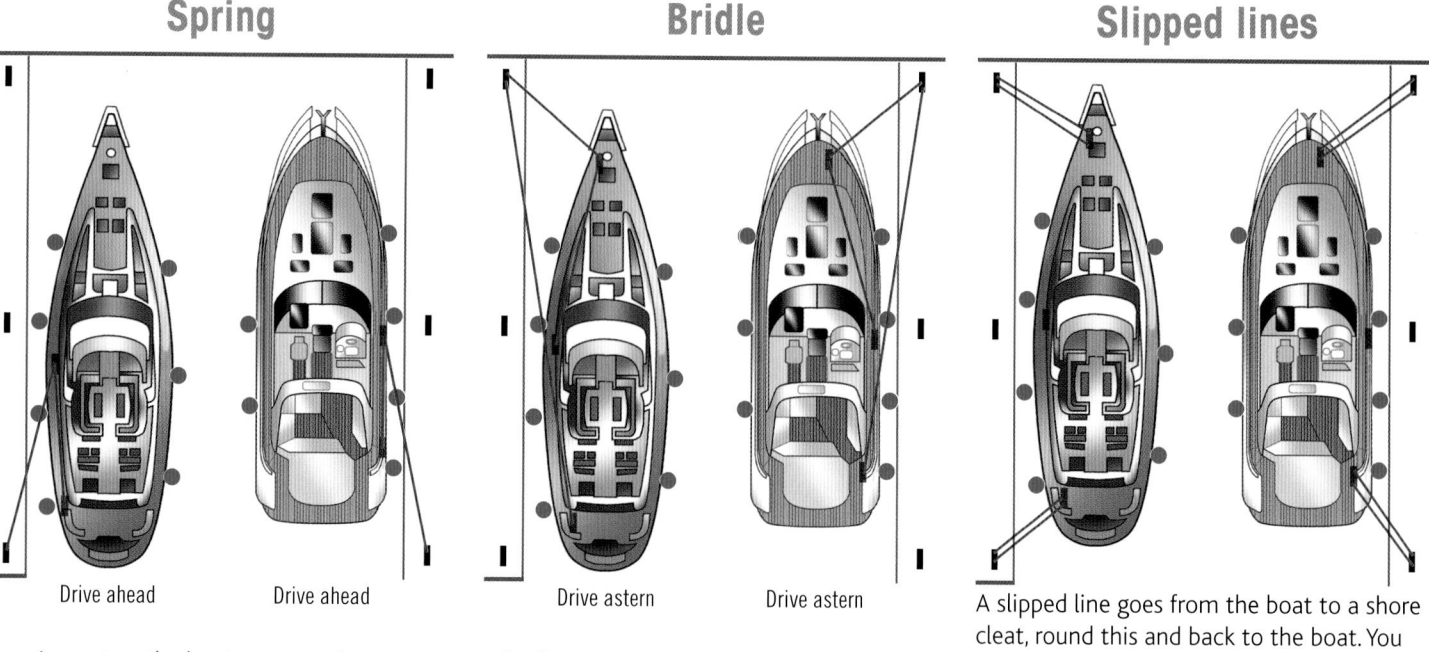

Spring

Drive ahead   Drive ahead

A spring enters the boat at one point.

Bridle

Drive astern   Drive astern

A bridle enters the boat at two points.

Slipped lines

A slipped line goes from the boat to a shore cleat, round this and back to the boat. You release this from on board.
You need the least amount of line to slip.

MIDSHIP SPRING TO HOLD ALONGSIDE

The shape of a yacht means you need the midship cleat to be on or abaft the beam when driving against a spring line. If it is forward of the beam, instead of holding alongside, driving ahead will kick the stern out.

For a flat-sided motorboat, it is less critical where the midship cleat is placed in order to lie alongside.

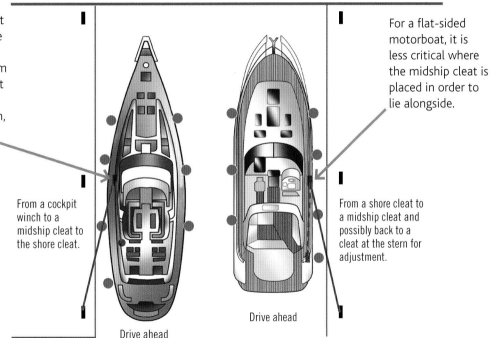

From a cockpit winch to a midship cleat to the shore cleat.

From a shore cleat to a midship cleat and possibly back to a cleat at the stern for adjustment.

Drive ahead

Drive ahead

Casting Off

MIDSHIP SPRING TO HOLD ALONGSIDE

Driving ahead against a midship spring, which holds the boat alongside.

Twin-engine boats use the inner engine only.

SPRINGING OUT THE STERN – SLIPPED LINE

- Run a line from a bow cleat to a shore cleat amidships and back set to slip.
- Fender up the bow well and drive ahead to bring the stern out – or use a stern thruster.
- Release the slipped line and reverse out into the tide.

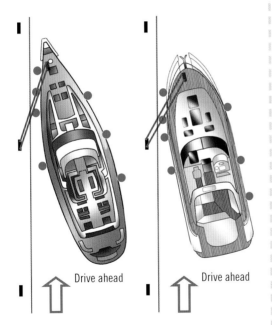

Drive ahead   Drive ahead

SPRINGING OUT THE BOW – SLIPPED LINE

- Run a line from a stern cleat to a shore cleat amidships and back set to slip.
- Fender up the stern well and drive astern to bring the bow out – or use a bow thruster.
- Release the slipped line and drive out into the tide.

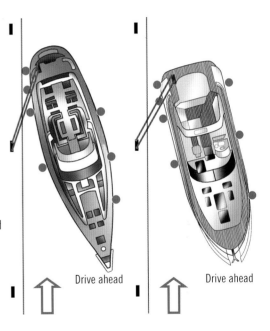

Drive ahead   Drive ahead

Casting Off

SPRINGING OUT THE BOW – SLIPPED LINE

Drive astern against a slipped line from the stern cleat to a cleat on shore amidships to spring the bow out into the tide.

Large fender to
protect stern

Large fender to
protect stern

DRIVING ASTERN AGAINST A SLIPPED BOW BRIDLE

- The bridle runs from a strong point (a winch) in the cockpit along the deck, inside the shrouds to a bow cleat.
- Down to the cleat on shore by the bow, round this.
- Back onboard amidships and secure on a cockpit winch.
- Click the boat into astern.
- Remove mooring lines – and electricity!
- To depart, release the bridle on the winch and haul in on the inboard end and the boat will drive astern out of the berth.

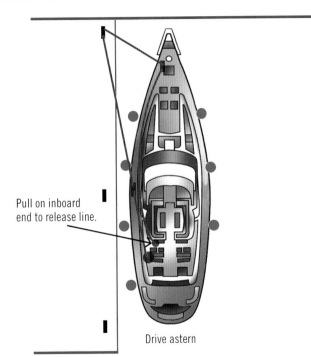

Pull on inboard end to release line.

Drive astern

Casting Off

BOW BRIDLE

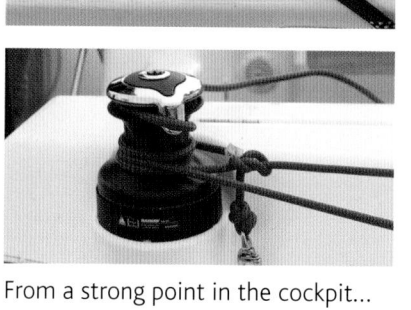

From a strong point in the cockpit...

(it could be the same winch on which you will secure the line)

Run the line inside the shrouds to the bow, down to the shore cleat and back on board amidships and secure on a winch.

Click the engine into astern and remove your mooring warps.

Make sure you have the least amount of line to slip.

To depart, release the line on the winch and haul in on the inboard end of the line.

DRIVING ASTERN AGAINST A SLIPPED BOW BRIDLE

- The bridle runs from a strong point (a midship or stern cleat) along the deck, to a bow cleat.
- Down to the cleat on shore by the bow, round this.
- Back onboard amidships and secure on the midship or stern cleat with a line set to slip.
- Click the boat into astern – inner engine for twin-engine boats.
- Remove mooring lines – and electricity!
- To depart, release the bridle from the cleat and haul in on the inboard end and the boat will drive astern out of the berth.

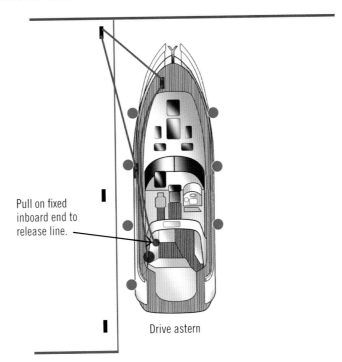

Pull on fixed inboard end to release line.

Drive astern

Casting Off

BOW BRIDLE

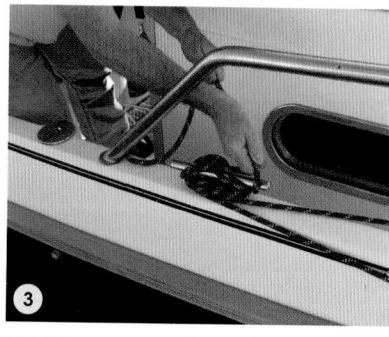

1. Attach a line to the cleat on the side deck...

2. Run the line along the deck to the bow, down to the shore cleat and back on board and secure with an OXO on the side.

3. Make sure you have the least amount of line to slip.

4. Click the engine into astern and remove your mooring warps.

5. To depart, release the line on the cleat and haul in on the inboard end.

REMOVABLE HEAD SPRING

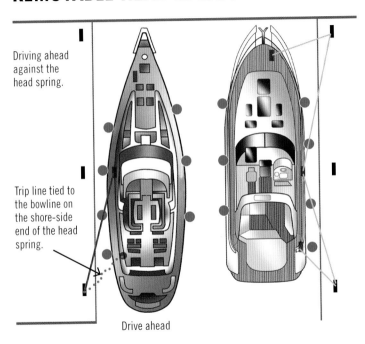

Driving ahead against the head spring.

Trip line tied to the bowline on the shore-side end of the head spring.

Drive ahead

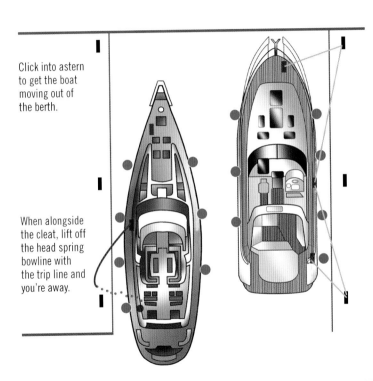

Click into astern to get the boat moving out of the berth.

When alongside the cleat, lift off the head spring bowline with the trip line and you're away.

Casting Off

REMOVABLE HEAD SPRING

1. If you use 4 lines to moor your boat, you can set up for an easy departure when you arrive.

2. With bowlines in the shore end of the line and the head spring under the stern line, attach another line, a 'trip' line, to the bowline of the head spring.

3. Drive against the head spring and remove the other lines. The boat will hold alongside to the head spring.

4. Engine into astern. Lift off the head spring.

5. And away you go...

REMOVABLE HEAD SPRING

Driving ahead against the head spring.

Trip line tied to the bowline on the shore-side end of the head spring.

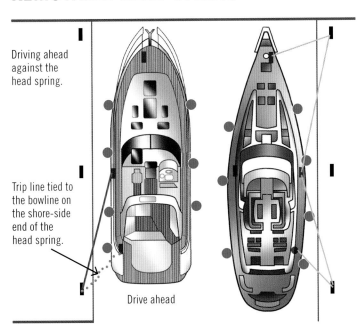

Drive ahead

Click into astern to get the boat moving out of the berth.

When alongside the cleat, lift off the head spring bowline with the trip line and you're away.

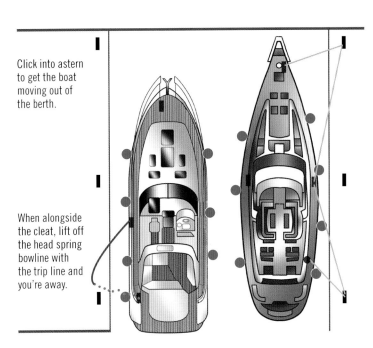

Casting Off

REMOVABLE HEAD SPRING

1. Driving against a head spring – inner engine if twin engine.

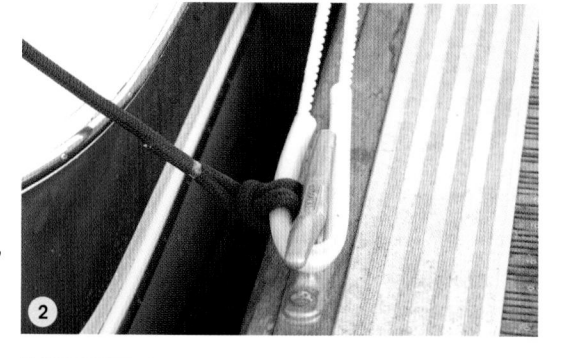

2. Attach a 'trip' line to the head spring bowline.

3. Engine into neutral.

4. Lift spring off cleat and you're away...

HEAD SPRING WITH RUSTLER'S HITCH

Driving ahead against a head spring secured to the cleat on shore with a rustler's hitch

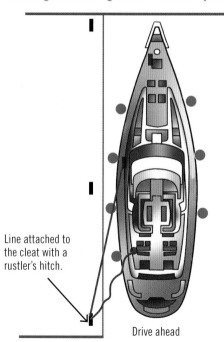

Line attached to the cleat with a rustler's hitch.

Drive ahead

Rustler's hitch – tied from seaward so it can be released from on board.

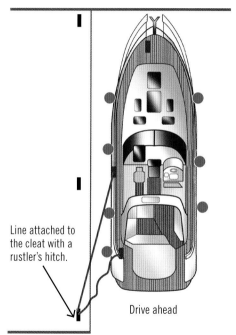

Line attached to the cleat with a rustler's hitch.

Drive ahead

Casting Off

HEAD SPRING WITH RUSTLER'S HITCH

- Rustler's hitch on to stern cleat ashore – tied from seaward.
- Standing end OXO'd to midship cleat with a locking hitch.
- Running end led on board.
- Click engine into ahead.
- Boat will hold alongside the dock.
- Remove mooring lines.

To depart:
- Engine into neutral.
- Sharp tug on the running end of the rustler's hitch to release it.
- Into astern and drive out of the berth.

HEAD SPRING WITH RUSTLER'S HITCH

- Rustler's hitch on to stern cleat ashore – tied from seaward.
- Standing end OXO'd to midship cleat with a locking hitch.
- Running end led on board.
- Click engine into ahead.
- Boat will hold alongside the dock.
- Remove mooring lines.

To depart:

- Engine into neutral.
- Sharp tug on the running end of the rustler's hitch to release it.
- Into astern and drive out of the berth.

Casting Off

STERN IN – SLIPPED STERN LINE

Aft cockpit

Centre cockpit

Drive ahead

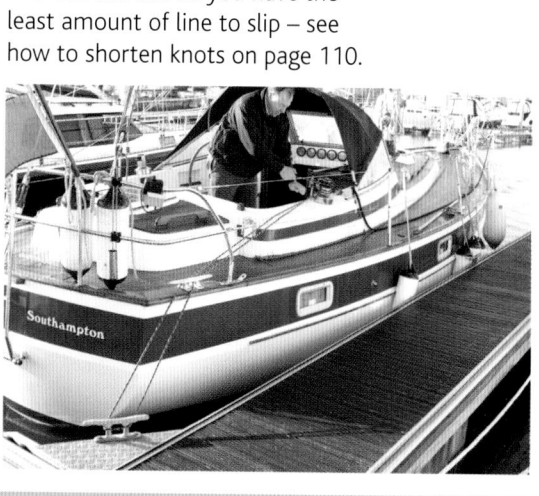

Shorten the line so you have the least amount of line to slip – see how to shorten knots on page 110.

STERN IN – SLIPPED STERN LINE

Drive ahead

On twin-engine boats always use the inner engine only, clicked into ahead. Using the outer engine can make the boat try to 'climb the dock'.

Shorten the line so you have the least amount of line to slip – see how to shorten knots on page 110.

With stern drives, you can balance them one ahead one astern so there is no tension in the slipped stern line.

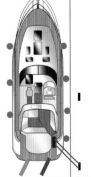

SSR 125177

Casting Off

A SLIPPED MIDSHIP LINE – BOWS IN OR STERN IN

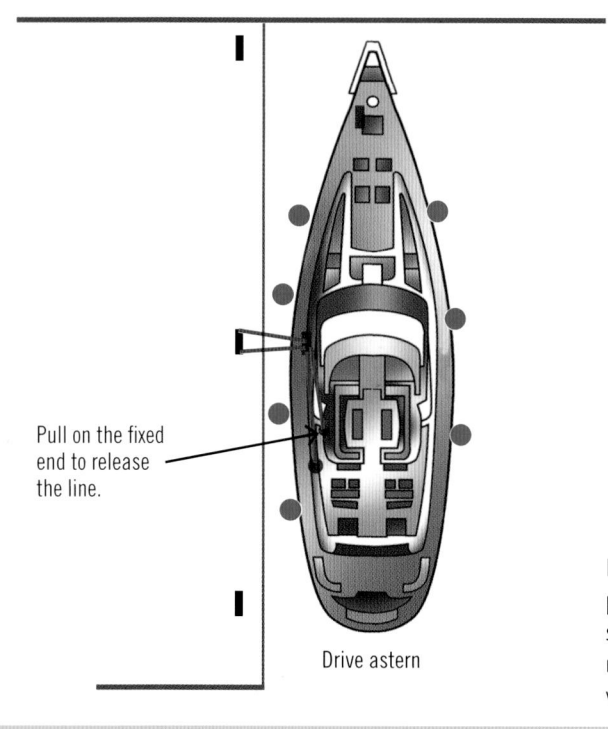

Pull on the fixed end to release the line.

Drive astern

Notice how the two parts of the line are kept separate so they don't rub against each other when you haul in.

A SLIPPED MIDSHIP LINE – BOWS IN OR STERN IN

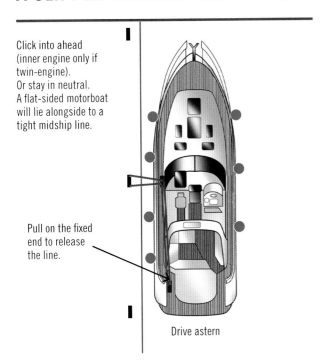

Click into ahead (inner engine only if twin-engine). Or stay in neutral. A flat-sided motorboat will lie alongside to a tight midship line.

Pull on the fixed end to release the line.

Drive astern

Parts of the slipped line are separated so as to reduce friction when releasing.

Flat-sided boats can hang quite happily off a midship line. This has not been led back to the cockpit.

Casting Off

DRIVING AHEAD AGAINST A SLIPPED STERN BRIDLE

To depart, put the engine into neutral, release the bridle on the winch, haul in on the inboard end and then into gear and drive out of the berth. You can also do this with the engine in gear ahead, especially if there is a wind that might blow you off the dock with the engine in neutral.

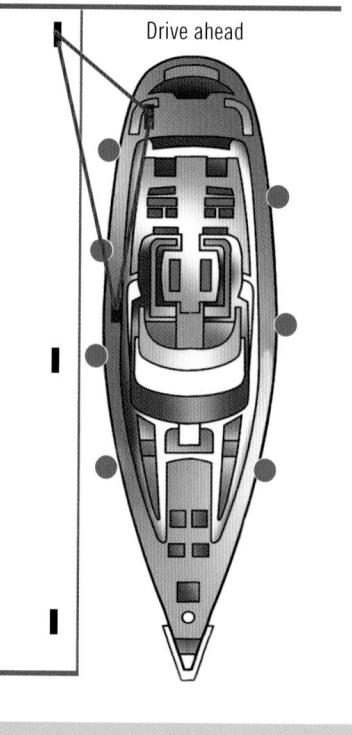

Drive ahead

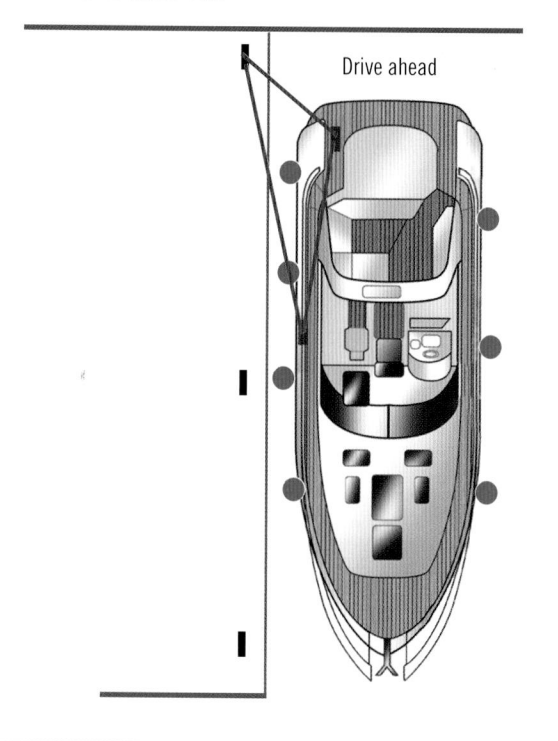

Drive ahead

STERN BRIDLE

The setup – from winch, round midship cleat then shore cleat and back to winch – drive ahead.

1. Our line is too long and needs to be shortened.

2. Measure the length required and make a loop in the line, here an Alpine Butterfly knot (see page 110).

3. Put the loop on the winch.

4. Run the line round the midship cleat to the shore cleat...

5. ...and back to the winch. Drive ahead.

6. To depart, take the line off the winch and haul in on the inboard end.

Casting Off

STERN BRIDLE

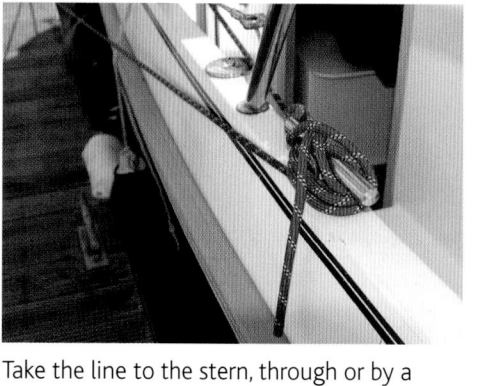

Make a loop in a line and place this over the midship cleat.

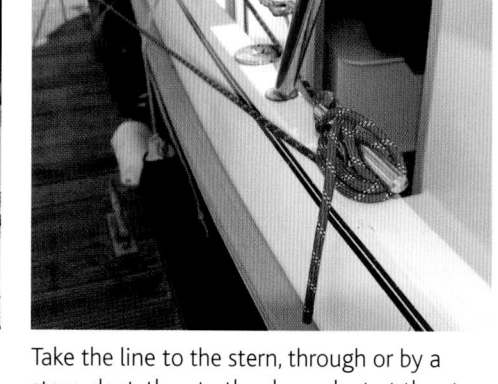

Take the line to the stern, through or by a stern cleat, then to the shore cleat at the stern and back amidships. OXO on the midship cleat, leaving as little line to slip as possible.

Drive ahead – twin-engine boats use inner engine – and remove mooring lines.

To depart, put engine into neutral, remove OXO and haul in on the inboard end of the line. With the line clear and on deck, click the engine into ahead and go.

SPRINGING OUT THE STERN – USING A RUSTLER'S HITCH

- Tie a rustler's hitch (see page 27) to a cleat on shore amidships, with the standing end taken to a cleat on the bow.
- Tension this and make fast on the bow cleat.
- Take the running end to the cockpit.
- Drive ahead.
- The bow will come into the dock.
- The stern will kick out into the tide.
- Before reversing out into the tide, release the rustler's hitch by pulling sharply on the running end.
- Use a winch if the line is difficult to free.

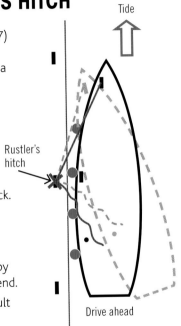

Tide

Rustler's hitch

Drive ahead

SPRINGING OUT THE BOW – USING A RUSTLER'S HITCH

- Tie a rustler's hitch to a cleat on shore amidships, with the standing end taken to a cleat at the stern.
- Tension this and make fast on the stern cleat.
- Take the running end to the cockpit.
- Drive astern.
- The stern will come into the dock.
- The bow will kick out into the tide.
- Before reversing out into the tide, release the rustler's hitch by pulling sharply on the running end.
- Use a winch if the line is difficult to free.

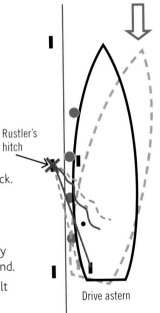

Tide

Rustler's hitch

Drive astern

Casting Off

Casting Off

SPRINGING OUT THE STERN – USING A RUSTLER'S HITCH

Rustler's hitch on a short cleat.

Standing end to bow cleat, running end to cockpit.

Drive ahead – bow comes in, stern goes out.

Release rustler's hitch – drive out astern into tide.

SPRINGING OUT THE BOW – USING A RUSTLER'S HITCH

Rustler's hitch on shore, spring to aft cleat.

Engine astern brings bow out – release rustler's hitch.

Gather up the line and return to the cockpit.

Drive out into the tide.

Casting Off

ALWAYS MOOR INTO THE TIDE FOR PERFECT CONTROL

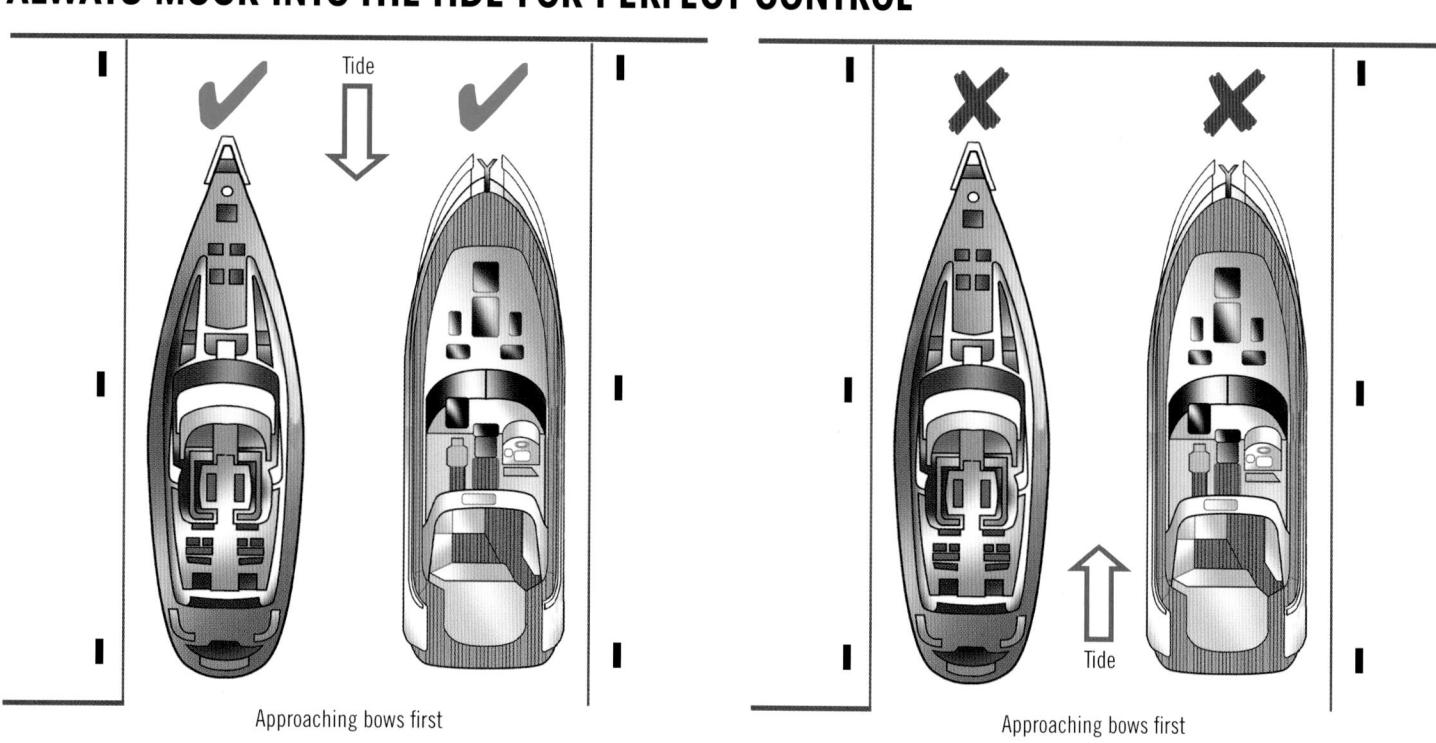

Approaching bows first

Approaching bows first

ALWAYS MOOR INTO THE TIDE FOR PERFECT CONTROL

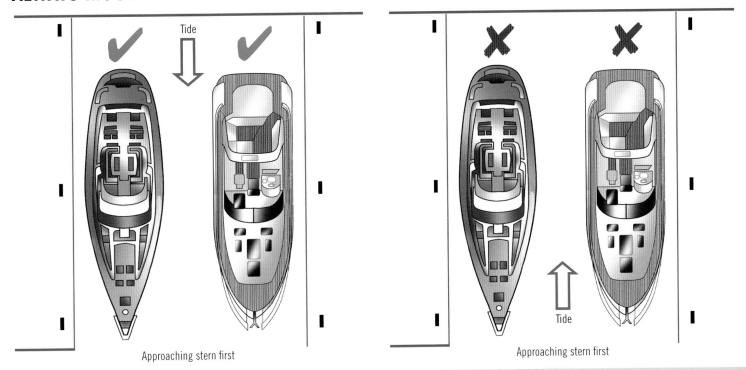

Tide

Approaching stern first

Tide

Approaching stern first

Coming Alongside

Coming Alongside

APPROACH 1 – WIND BLOWING ON – AIM HIGH

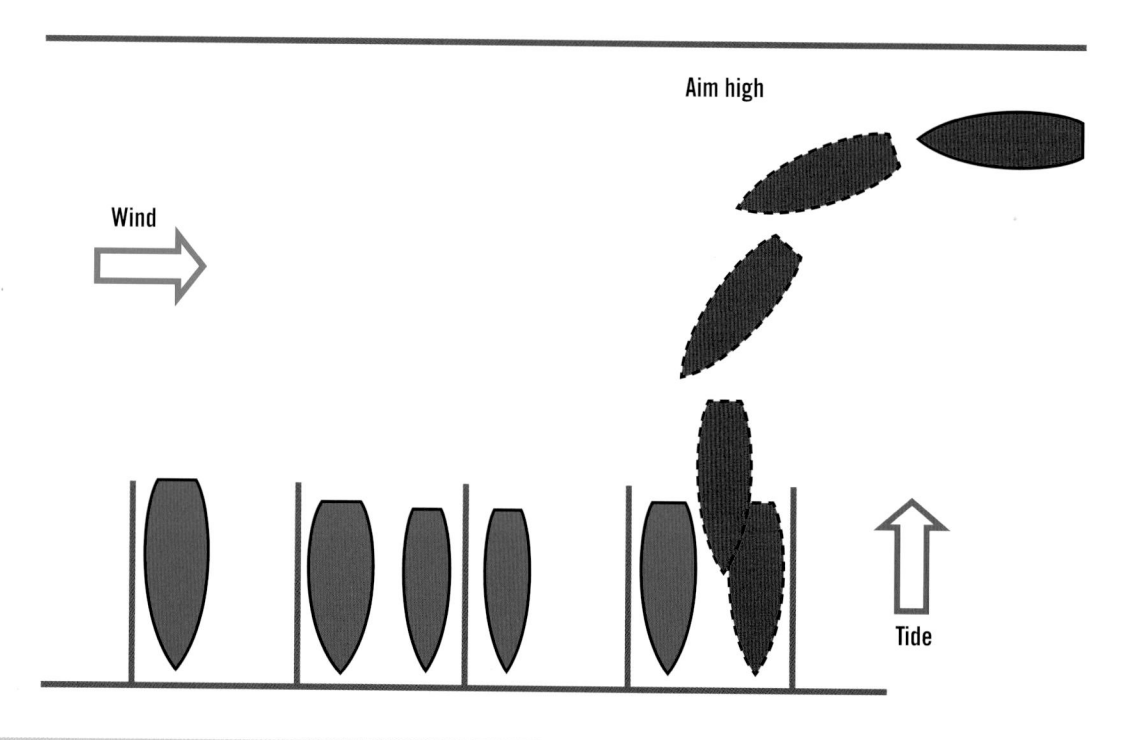

Aim high

Wind

Tide

APPROACH 2 – WIND BLOWING OFF – TURN INTO WIND

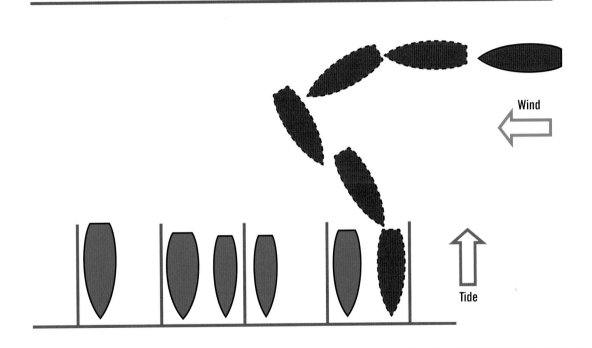

Wind

Tide

Coming Alongside

BOWS IN – STERN BRIDLE

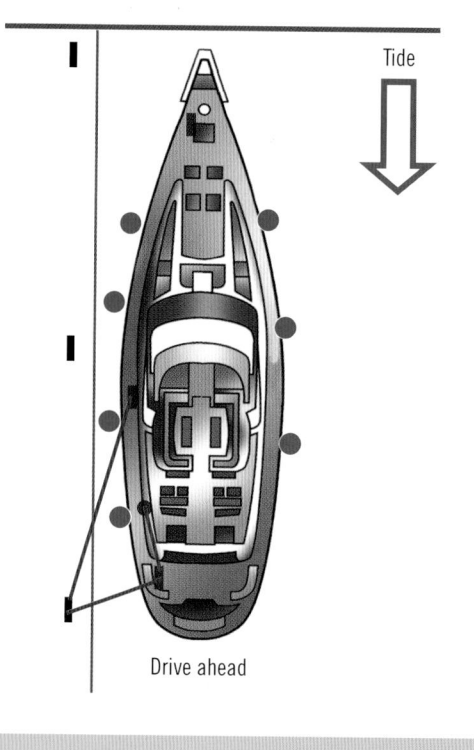

Tide

Drive ahead

- Attach the bridle to a midship cleat.
- Take it outside everything and bring it on board at the stern and up to a cockpit winch.
- Allow enough line to make 4 coils to lasso the cleat.
- Place the coils carefully in the cockpit.
- Approach the berth. Stop the boat. Lasso the cleat.
- Take up the slack, secure the line and drive ahead against it. The boat will come alongside.

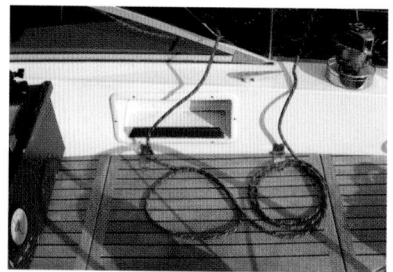

BOWS IN – STERN BRIDLE

At no point with any of the following techniques do you use the cleat to take way off the boat. The boat must be stopped alongside the cleat before you lasso it.

1. Stop the boat. Lasso the end cleat on the pontoon.

Tide

2. Haul in the slack.

3. Secure the bridle on the cleat.

4. Click the engine into ahead.

5. The boat will come into the dock and stay there.

Coming Alongside

BOWS IN – STERN BRIDLE

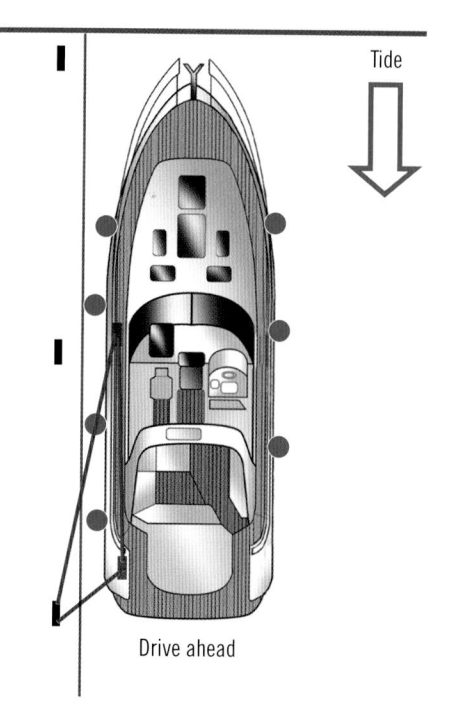

Tide

Drive ahead

- Attach the bridle to a midship cleat.
- Take it outside everything and bring it on board at the stern through the centre of a stern cleat to keep it safe.
- Allow enough line to make 4 coils to lasso the cleat.
- Place the coils carefully in the cockpit.
- Approach the berth. Stop the boat. Lasso the cleat.
- Take up the slack, secure the line and drive ahead against it. The boat will come alongside.

BOWS IN – STERN BRIDLE

At no point with any of the following techniques do you use the cleat to take way off the boat. The boat must be stopped alongside the cleat before you lasso it.

1. Driving into the tide or current, stop the boat.

Tide ⟹

2. Lasso the shore cleat or bollard.

Notice the line led through the centre of the cleat to keep it safe.

3. Haul in the slack.

4. Make fast on the cleat and then click into ahead.

Coming Alongside

STERN TO – LASSO A SHORE CLEAT WITH A STERN LINE OR STERN BRIDLE

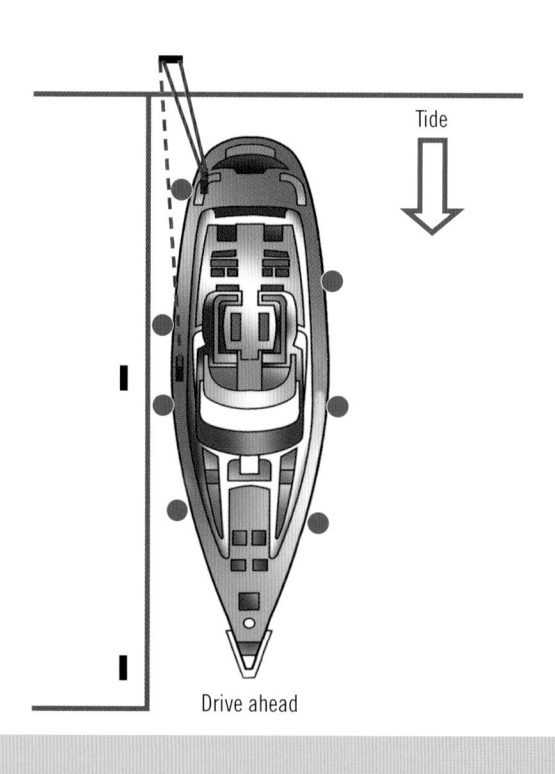

Tide

Drive ahead

Stern line.

Stern bridle.

STERN TO – LASSO A SHORE CLEAT WITH A STERN LINE OR STERN BRIDLE

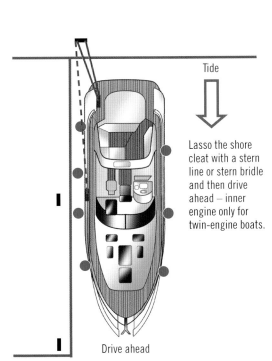

Drive ahead

Tide

Lasso the shore cleat with a stern line or stern bridle and then drive ahead – inner engine only for twin-engine boats.

Stern line.

Stern bridle.

1. Make a loop of a short piece of line with a double fisherman's knot. Drop it over the shore cleat and round the cleat on board.

2. Drive ahead against this and the boat will lie alongside – use inner engine.

Coming Alongside

A MIDSHIP LINE

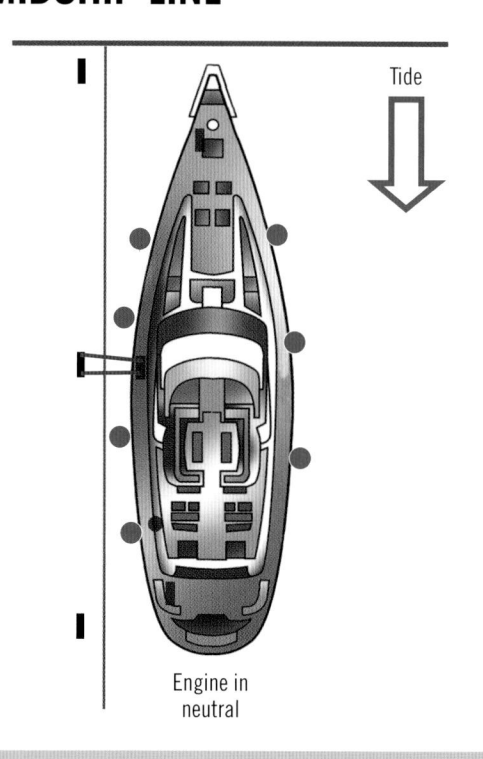

Tide

Engine in neutral

- Tie a bowline in the end of a line.
- Pass the bowline through the middle of the centre cleat and over the wings.
- Make 4 coils.
- When alongside and stopped, lasso the cleat.
- Haul in the line tight and make fast to the cleat with an OXO and a hitch, if you like.

The boat will lie alongside. There is no need to drive against the line.

A MIDSHIP LINE

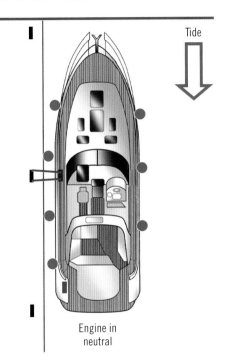

Tide

Engine in neutral

- Tie a bowline in the end of a line.
- Pass the bowline through the middle of the centre cleat and over the wings.
- Make 4 coils.
- When alongside and stopped, lasso the cleat.
- Haul in the line tight and make fast to the cleat with an OXO and a hitch, if you like.

The boat will lie alongside. There is no need to drive against the line.

Coming Alongside

SHORT FINGER BERTH – T-CLEAT AT END – BOWS TO

Use a stern bridle. Bring the return point of the bridle at the stern further forward. This point will line up with the cleat on the finger.

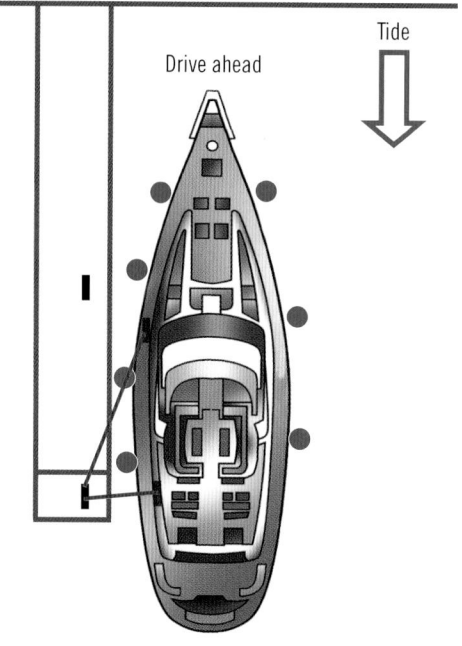

Drive ahead

Tide

The bridle returns to the boat much further forward as it runs through a block on the Genoa sheet lead track.

Stern bridle.

SHORT FINGER BERTH – BAR AT END –T-CLEAT HALFWAY DOWN FINGER – BOWS TO

Set a stern bridle and lasso the entire finger, or set a midship spring and grab the bar with a snap hook. I have also used a 'toy' grapnel anchor dropped between the bar and the pontoon set as a midship spring.

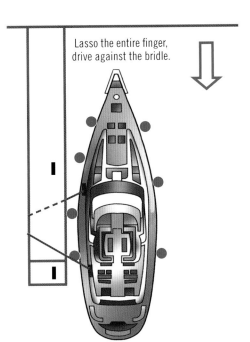

Lasso the entire finger, drive against the bridle.

Finger lassoed, driving against the bridle.

Toy grapnel anchor.

Line through the midship cleat, drive against the 'spring'. Ease the spring until you are in position and set mooring lines.

Coming Alongside

SHORT FINGER BERTH – BAR AT END – SHORESIDE T-CLEAT – STERN TO

Lasso the cleat on shore using a stern line or a stern bridle, drive against this to hold alongside.

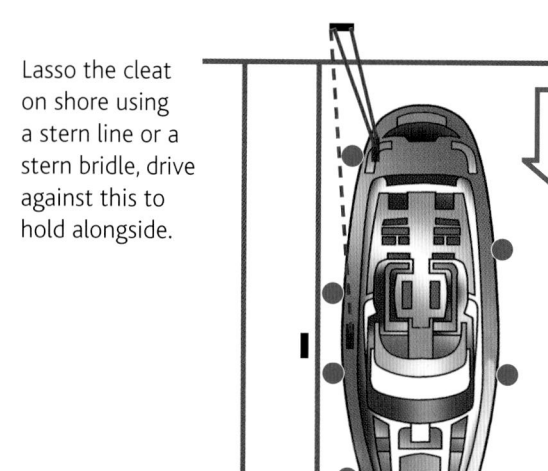

Drive ahead

Stern line.

Short French finger berths.

Lasso the shoreside cleat.

Stern bridle.

SHORT FINGER BERTH – BAR AT END – SHORESIDE T-CLEAT – STERN TO

Lasso the shoreside T-cleat with a stern line or stern bridle and then drive ahead.

Inner engine only for twin-engine boats.

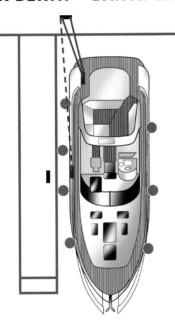

Drive ahead

Short French finger berths.

Lasso the shoreside cleat.

Stern line.

Stern bridle.

Coming Alongside

NO T-CLEATS, NO BOLLARDS, JUST CHAINS, HOOPS, BARS OR RINGS

Use a device such as a snap hook (carabiner) on the end of a pole or boathook and whack it at the bar or hoop. If picking up a mooring ring, select one of the makes that holds the gate of the hook open.

Hoop?

Bar?

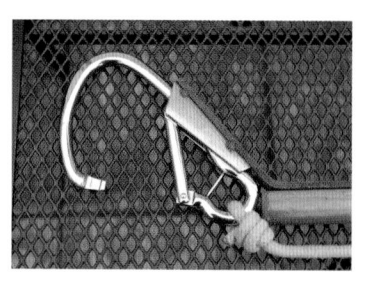

Use a device like a snap hook.

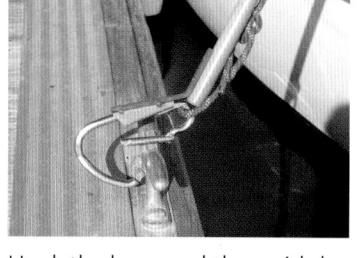

Hook the hoop and then withdraw the pole.

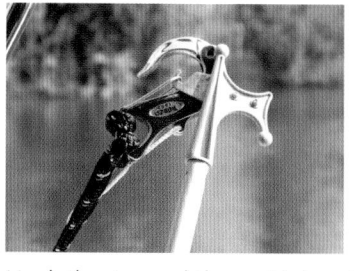

Hook the ring and then withdraw the boathook.

NO T-CLEATS, NO BOLLARDS, JUST CHAINS, HOOPS, BARS OR RINGS

Chain? Use a snap hook, which holds the gate open, to grab hold of the chain – or wait for one of the restaurant people to help you.

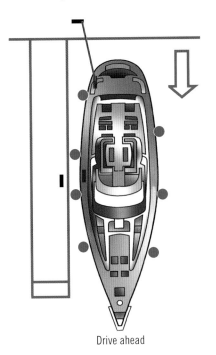

Drive ahead

Chain? Use a snap hook.

Coming Alongside

NO T-CLEATS, NO BOLLARDS, JUST HOOPS, BARS OR RINGS

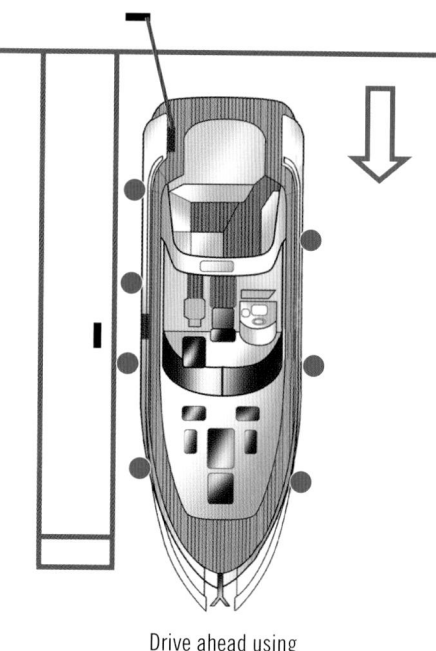

Drive ahead using
the inner engine

Use a device such as a snap hook on a removable pole to grab the hoop, bar or ring, secure the line on board and drive against the line or spring – use the inner engine for twin-engine boats.

MED MOORING –
STERN TO UNDER ANCHOR

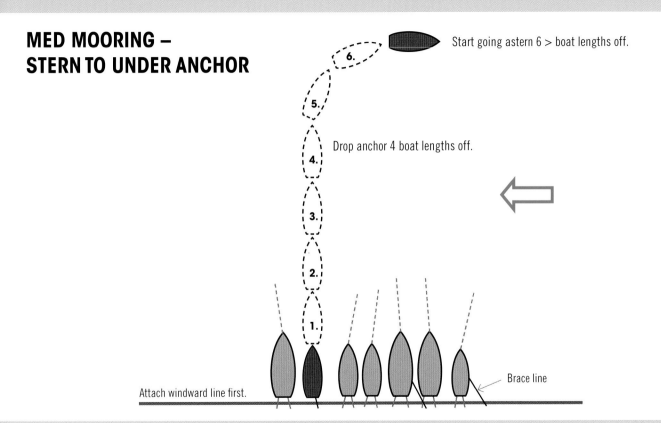

Start going astern 6 > boat lengths off.

Drop anchor 4 boat lengths off.

Attach windward line first.

Brace line

Coming Alongside

Coming Alongside

MED MOORING – STERN TO UNDER ANCHOR – STRONG CROSSWIND

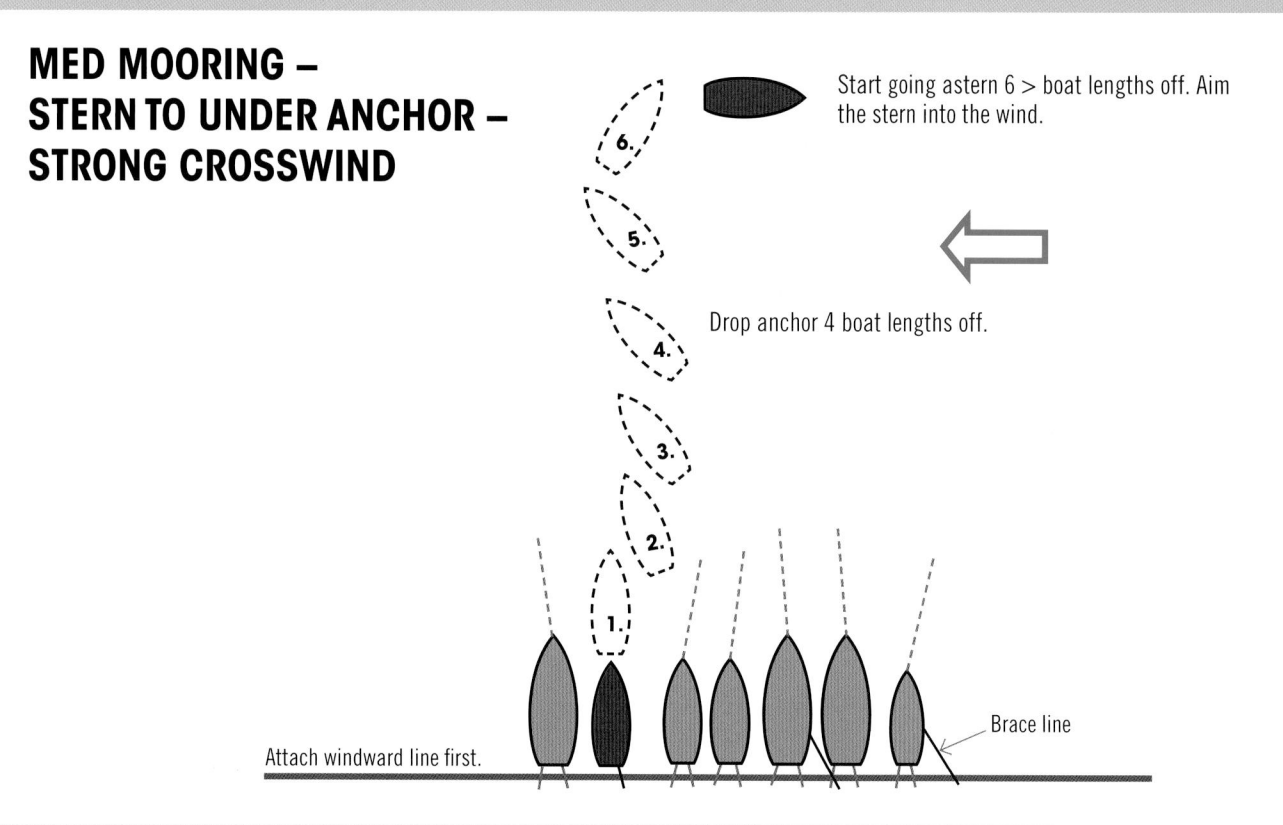

Start going astern 6 > boat lengths off. Aim the stern into the wind.

Drop anchor 4 boat lengths off.

Brace line

Attach windward line first.

BOX MOORING – OPTIONS

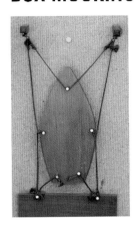

1. Lie alongside the posts first.

2. Then pick up the windward line first and warp the boat in.

3. Or get a spring on the windward post.

4. Then back the boat in against it.

Coming Alongside

BOX MOORING SINGLEHANDED WITH A BRIDLE RUNNING FROM BOW TO STERN

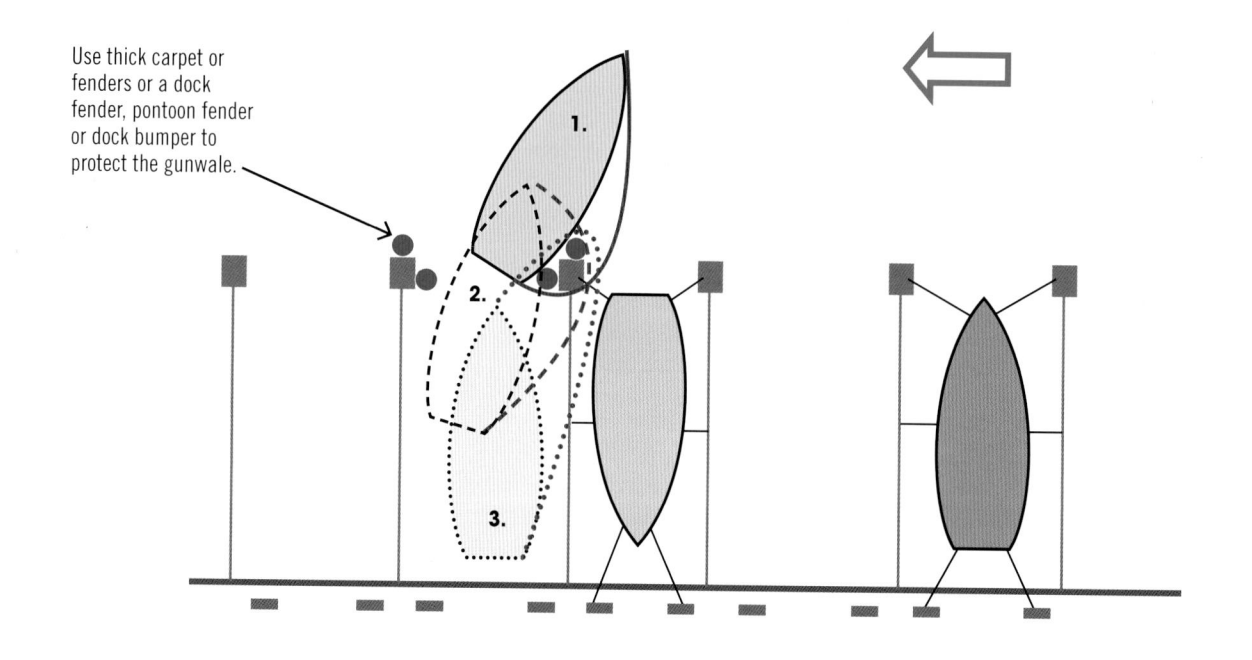

Use thick carpet or fenders or a dock fender, pontoon fender or dock bumper to protect the gunwale.

RAFTING UP

- Approach the host boat into the tide.
- Fenders set at gunwale height.
- If possible, attach a short midship line between the two of you.
- Hand the host crew lines with bowlines tied in them so they can place these round their cleat. You adjust at your end.
- After setting bow and stern lines and springs, remember to set shore lines fore and aft.

1. A fender set at pontoon height when taken under the lower guard wire and over the upper becomes a fender set at gunwale height.

3. Hand the host crew lines with bowlines tied to the ends.

2. Set a tight midship line to stop you drifting back with the tide before handing the host crew lines.

4. Notice here how fenders set on the boat with the lower gunwale are not protecting her from the gunwale of the host boat. Always set fenders from the boat with the higher topsides first.

Rafting Up/Leaving a Raft

LEAVING A RAFT – how to leave from the middle of a raft

- Follow the colours of the lines to see what each boat has set at each stage.

- **Stage 3**: Boat 2 sets a slipped back spring from a midship cleat on Boat 1 to a stern cleat on Boat 2 and drives astern against this to spring the bow out, slips the spring and departs.

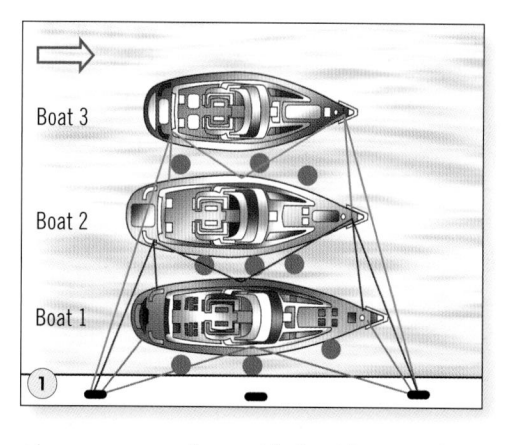

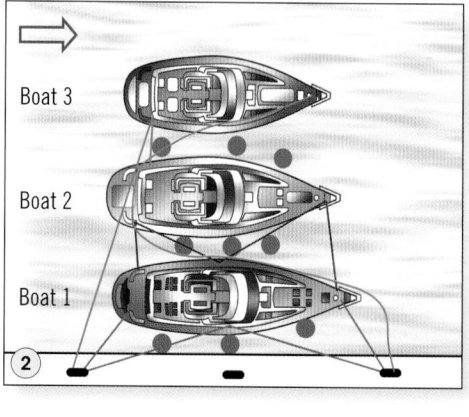

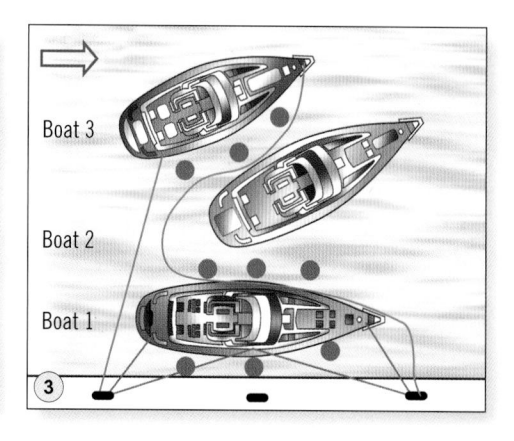

Always open a raft up with the tide, never into it. That way, the tide will close the raft up once the boat has left.

RAFTING UP AND LEAVING A RAFT – how to leave from the middle of a raft

- Approach the host boat into the tide.
- Fenders set at gunwale height.
- If possible, attach a short midship line between the two of you.

- Hand the host crew lines with bowlines tied in them so they can place these round their cleat. You adjust at your end.
- Set your mooring lines and lines to the shore.

- Follow the colours of the lines to see what each boat has set at each stage.
- In **Stage 3**, Boat 2 springs off Boat 1 to get her bow out and open the raft before departing.

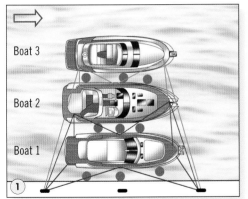

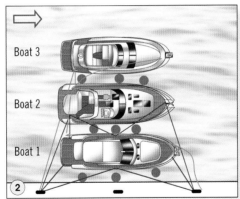

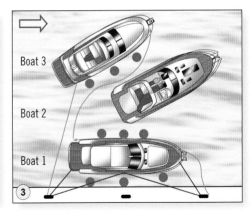

Always open a raft up with the tide, never into it. That way, the tide will close the raft up once the boat has left.

Rafting Up/Leaving a Raft

ANCHORING AND ANCHORS

Anchoring

- To lie to one anchor is to be anchored.
- To lie to two anchors, as in a Bahamian moor, is to be moored.

Anchors

- The bower anchor – the main anchor that you deploy from the bow.
- Kedge anchor – a spare anchor that you would deploy in a dinghy and use to kedge off a sandbank, often a Fortress or CQR.

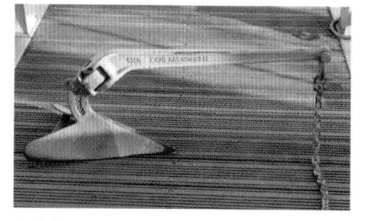
CQR/Plough.

Delta.

Rocna.

Fortress.

Lash the anchor to the boat when not in use.

Grapnel.

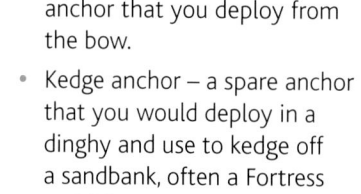
Bruce.

FIVE ESSENTIALS OF ANCHORING

SHELTER
- Not a lee shore, or likely to become one, no nasty tides.

NOT PROHIBITED
- Not a fairway, not a shipping lane, not restricted/prohibited.

HOLDING
- Will the bottom give good holding for your type of anchor?
- Mud and sand good, rock not always so good.

DEPTH
- Enough depth at low water and enough chain/rope at high water.

SWINGING
- Is there room to swing when the tide turns or if you are blown about by the breeze?

SCOPE

- 4 × depth for chain.
- 6 × depth for warp.
- With rope (warp), the first 10 metres need to be chain to help the anchor set.
- When calculating depth, allow for draught of boat if the echo sounder is giving you under-keel clearance and always allow a good metre from the water to the bow roller.

Anchoring

CALIBRATE THE CHAIN

Always know how much cable (chain/chain and rope) you are laying out.

My system? Coloured silks tied into the chain.

Anchor buddies		
The order you pot the snooker balls		
Red	=	5m
Yellow	=	10m
Green	=	15m
Brown	=	20m
Blue	=	25m
Pink	=	30m
Black	=	35m
2 × Red	=	40m
2 × Yellow	=	45m

Not a snooker fan?		
Run the colours alphabetically		
Black	=	5m
Blue	=	10m
Brown	=	15m
Green	=	20m
Pink	=	25m
Red	=	30m
Yellow	=	35m
2 × Black	=	40m
2 × Blue	=	45m

GETTING THE ANCHOR DOWN IN A HURRY – VERTICAL WINDLASS

Need to stop the boat quickly?
Forget using the remote control.
Unlock the gypsy with the
locking lever or the key, and let
it run free, or...

*Always keep the
locking lever or
gypsy key in the
anchor locker.*

1. Unlash the anchor.

2. The tension on the chain will be too
great to lift it off the gyspy.

3. So pull the chain out of the locker from
the back of the gypsy.

4. Lift the chain off the gypsy and pay
it out.

Anchoring

GETTING THE ANCHOR DOWN IN A HURRY – HORIZONTAL WINDLASS

Need to stop the boat quickly? Forget using the remote control. Unlock the gypsy with the locking lever or key, and let it run free, or...

Always keep the locking lever or gypsy key in the anchor locker.

1. Unlash the anchor. The tension on the chain will be too great to pull it away from the gypsy.

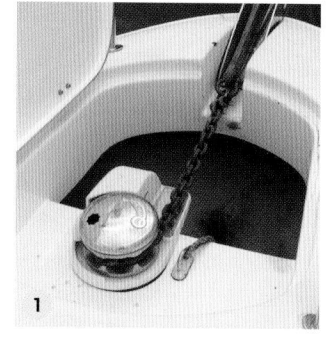

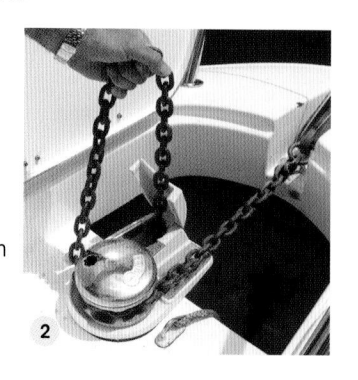

2. So pull the chain out of the locker from the back of the gypsy.

3. Pull the chain away from the gypsy and pay it out.

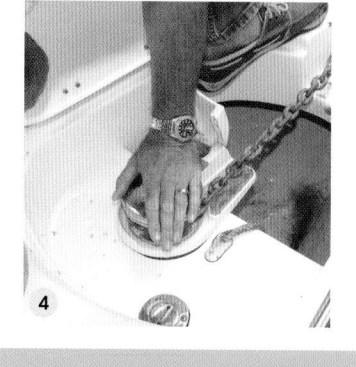

4. Sometimes a firm hand or foot on the locking plate can undo it (keep fingers away from the chain).

ANCHOR STUCK?

- Try driving the boat over the anchor.
- Try driving the boat around and lifting the anchor from different angles.
- Take a sinking line, weight it, tie a loose bowline round the anchor chain. Allow this to drop to the bottom. The idea is to get this over the shaft/shank of the anchor and allow you to pull the anchor out backwards.
- If it won't come up, mark the spot by hitting the MOB button on the GPS and attach a buoy to the chain so you can find the anchor when you come back with a team of divers.
- If you think the bottom may be foul ground – don't anchor there in the first place. But if you have no choice, and have to anchor in an emergency, then set a tripping line to the tripping eye on the anchor, with a buoy to show where the anchor is. If the anchor becomes stuck, you can pull it out from the crown with the tripping line.

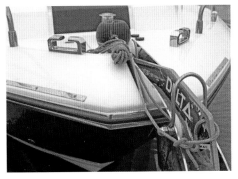

Anchoring

THE FISHERMAN'S TRICK

Fishermen often attach the chain to the tripping eye and then bind the chain to the shank with fishing line or cable ties. If the anchor gets stuck, then simply drive over it, break the line or ties and pull it out backwards.

I wouldn't use the system if you intend to have a sleep while anchored, just in case!

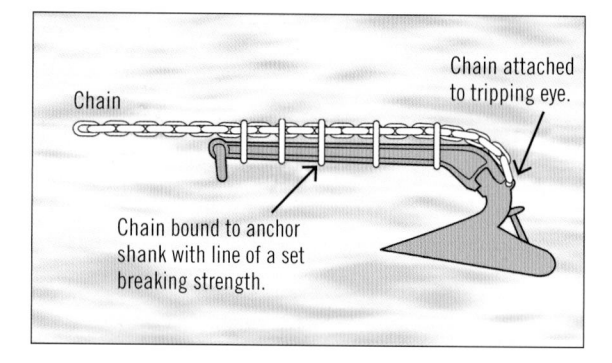

Chain

Chain attached to tripping eye.

Chain bound to anchor shank with line of a set breaking strength.

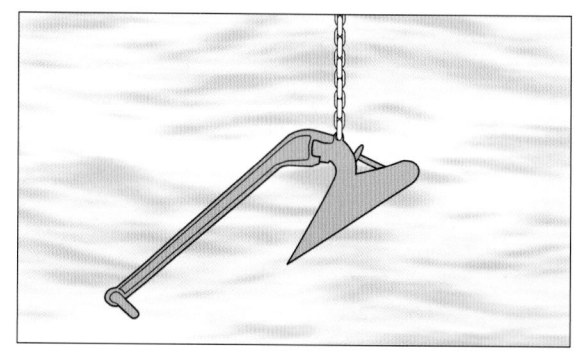

TRIPPING LINE

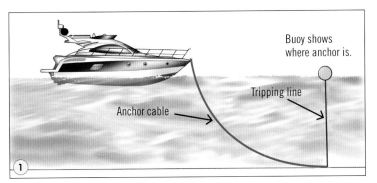

Buoy shows where anchor is.

Tripping line

Anchor cable

(1)

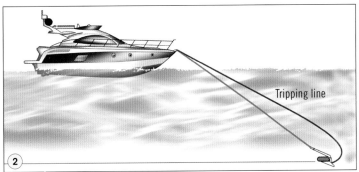

Tripping line

(2)

Tripping line

(3)

Tripping line

(4)

Anchoring

Picking Up a Mooring Buoy

MOORING BUOY – PENDANT AND PICK-UP FLOAT – BRIDLE – COCKPIT

Set a bridle from a bow cleat outside everything and bring it on board by the cockpit and secure on a winch

1. Into the tide, to leeward of the buoy with the pick-up float alongside the cockpit and the boat stopped in the water...

2. Pick up the float with the boathook.

3. Thread the bridle through the eye of the pendant...

4. And secure on the winch.

5. The buoy will now make its way to the bow.

6. A little astern will encourage it.

7. Walk to the bow...

8. And secure the eye of the pendant on a bow cleat – moored!

Over running the mooring buoy? Set a kedge anchor from the stern.

MOORING BUOY – PENDANT AND PICK-UP FLOAT – BRIDLE – AMIDSHIPS

Set a bridle from a bow cleat outside everything and bring it on board amidships

1. Approach into the tide to leeward of the buoy.

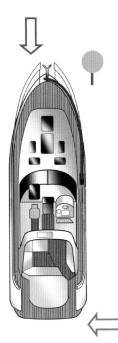

2. Grab the pick-up float with the boat hook. Thread the bridle through the eye of the pendant and secure the bridle on the midship cleat.

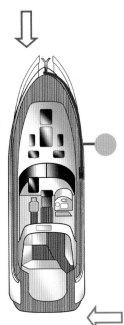

3. The boat will drift back with the tide and the buoy will make its way to the bow. To assist, click the leeward engine, here the port engine, into astern. This will move the boat astern and turn the stern towards the wind and help the buoy reach the bow. Place the eye of the pendant over a bow cleat.

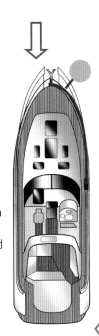

Picking Up a Mooring Buoy

MOORING BUOY – PENDANT AND PICK-UP FLOAT – BRIDLE – COCKPIT

Set a bridle from a bow cleat outside everything and bring it on board at the stern

1. Approach into the tide to leeward of the buoy.

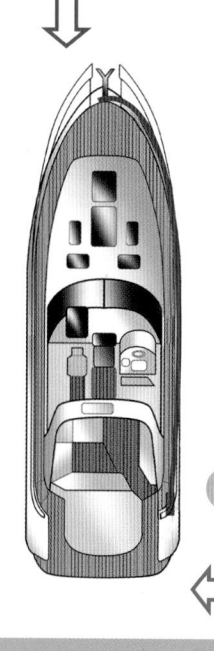

2. Grab the pick-up float with the boat hook. Thread the bridle through the eye of the pendant and secure the bridle on the stern cleat.

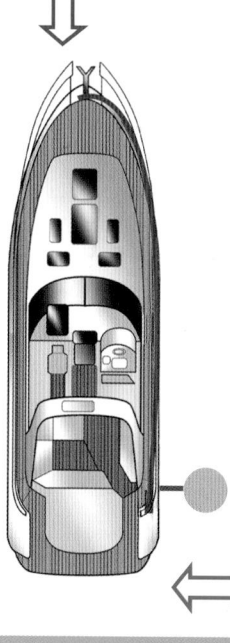

3. The boat will drift back with the tide and the buoy will make its way to the bow. To assist, click the leeward engine, here the port engine, into astern. This will move the boat astern and turn the stern towards the wind and help the buoy reach the bow. Place the eye of the pendant over a bow cleat.

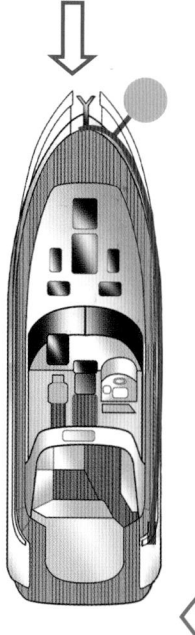

MOORING BUOY – PENDANT AND PICK-UP FLOAT – BRIDLE – COCKPIT

Bring it on board by the cockpit and secure on a stern cleat

1. Into the tide, to leeward of the buoy, stopped alongside...

2. Pick up the float.

3. Thread the bridle through the eye of the pendant...

4. And secure on a cleat.

5. The buoy will now make its way to the bow.

6. A little astern will encourage it.

7. Notice how the bow bridle has been led through the centre of the cleat to stop it sliding along the gunwale and putting any strain on any of the stanchions.

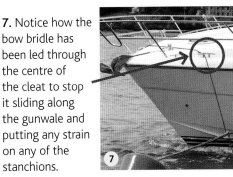

When ready to moor, place the eye of the pendant over the bow cleat.

Picking Up a Mooring Buoy

Picking Up a Mooring Buoy

MOORING BUOY – NO PENDANT – LASSO – COCKPIT

Set a bridle from a bow cleat outside everything and bring it on board by the cockpit and secure on a winch.

1. Approach into the tide, to leeward of the buoy, and bring the buoy amidships, or alongside the cockpit with the boat stopped in the water.

2. Fix the line to the bow cleat at one end and to a cockpit winch at the other with enough to make 4 coils to lasso and with 2 coils in either hand.

3. Throw the lasso high and wide.

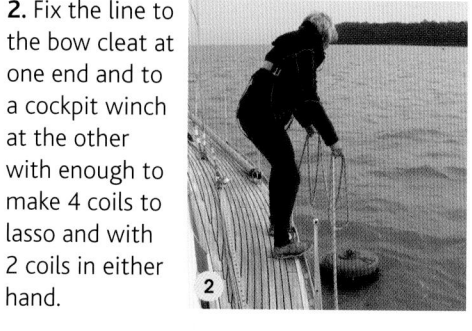

4. Allow the line to sink under the buoy before taking up the slack on the winch.

5. The buoy will now make its way to the bow.

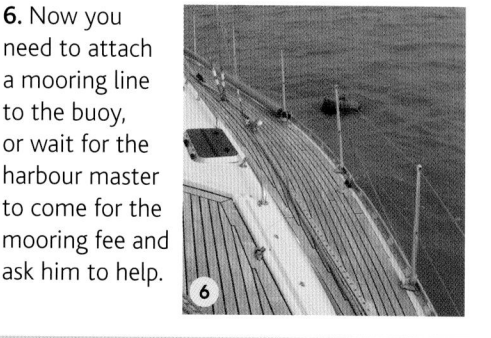

6. Now you need to attach a mooring line to the buoy, or wait for the harbour master to come for the mooring fee and ask him to help.

MOORING BUOY – NO PENDANT – LASSO – AMIDSHIPS

Set a line to a bow cleat outside everything and stand amidships by the helm ready to lasso

1. Approach into the tide, to leeward of the buoy.

2. With the boat stopped alongside the buoy and with short coils...

3. Throw high and wide and lasso the buoy. Keep hold of the running end!

4. Allow the lasso to sink under the buoy. Try not to lasso the buoy from above. Allow a lateral element to the lasso – this will help.

5. The boat will drop back with the tide and the buoy will make its way to the bow.

6. Now get out the dinghy and set a line to the ring on the buoy, or wait for the harbour master to come for the mooring fee and ask him to help.

Picking Up a Mooring Buoy

MOORING BUOY – NO PENDANT – STRONG TIDE – LASSO – COCKPIT

Set a bridle from a bow cleat outside everything and bring it on board by the cockpit and secure on a winch

1. When the buoy has its own bow wave, you are going to need something weightier than a simple line.

2. 1 metre of chain in a tube should be heavy enough. With a rope attached to either end of the chain, you also now have a loop – no end to lose!

3. Drop the heavy-duty lasso...

4. Over the buoy.

5. Take the slack out of the line. The buoy will make its way to the bow.

6. Now you need to attach a mooring line to the buoy, or wait for the harbour master to come for the mooring fee and ask him to help.

APPROACHING MOORING BUOYS

1. Crosswind – stern into the wind, drive up to the buoy on its downtide side.

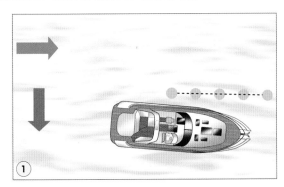

2. Wind on shoulder – stern into wind, drive up to the buoy on its downtide side.

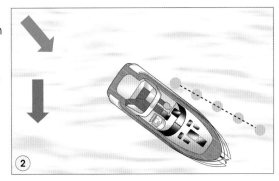

3. Wind on quarter – stern into wind, drive up to the buoy on its downtide side.

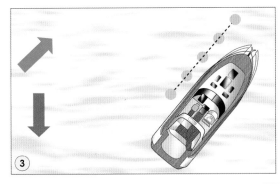

4. Wind on the nose – stern into wind, drive up to the buoy on its uptide side. This requires care.

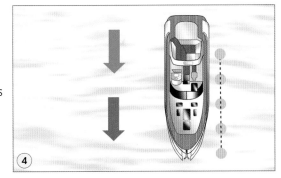

Picking Up a Mooring Buoy

SLIPPING THE MOORING – FROM THE COCKPIT

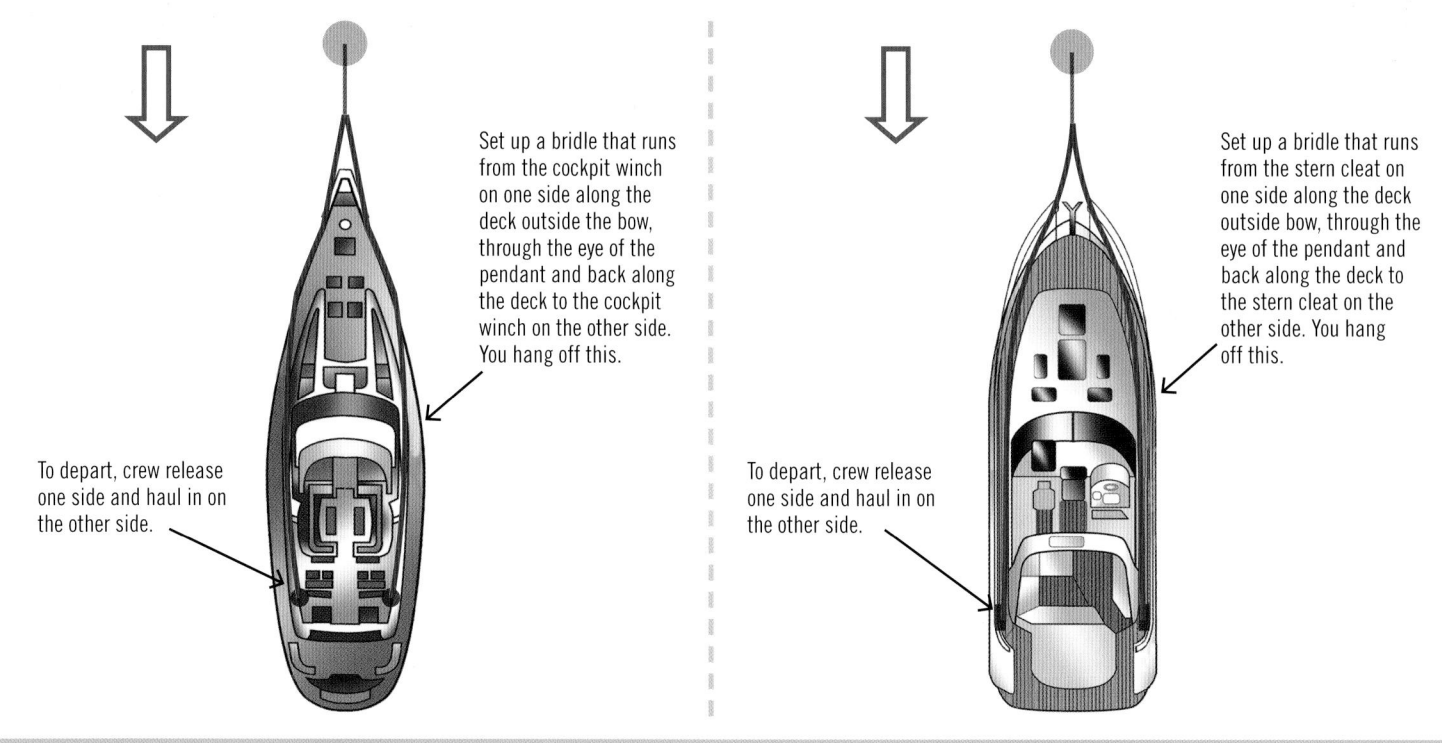

Set up a bridle that runs from the cockpit winch on one side along the deck outside the bow, through the eye of the pendant and back along the deck to the cockpit winch on the other side. You hang off this.

To depart, crew release one side and haul in on the other side.

Set up a bridle that runs from the stern cleat on one side along the deck outside bow, through the eye of the pendant and back along the deck to the stern cleat on the other side. You hang off this.

To depart, crew release one side and haul in on the other side.

SETTING UP FOR A SINGLEHANDED DEPARTURE

1. Set up a bridle from the cockpit on one side of the boat out past the stemhead, through the eye of the pendant, and back to the cockpit on the other side, and hang off this.

2. Make sure the bridle runs down inside the shrouds along the deck.

3. Release one end of the bridle and pull in on the other.

4. Depart, making sure all the bridle line is on board.

Picking Up a Mooring Buoy

BOWLINE AND SLIPKNOT

Bowline

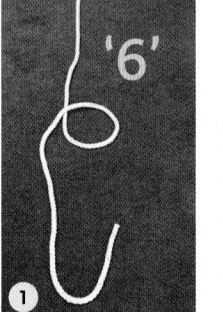

1. Draw a '6' in the line.

2. Take the working end, the running end, or the 'rabbit', up through the hole...

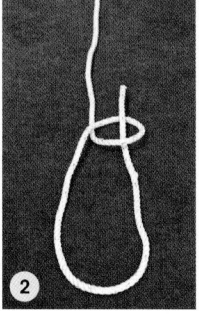

3. Round the back of the tree...

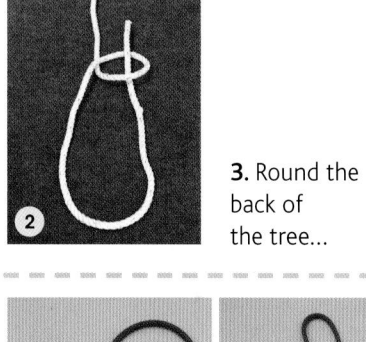

4. And back down the hole and tighten.

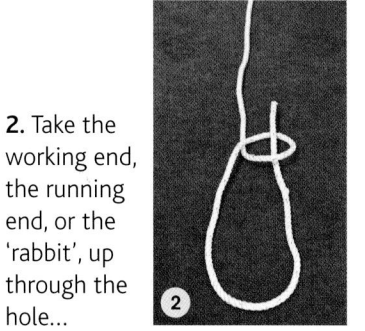

Slipknot

1. Cross the running end over the standing end to make a bight.

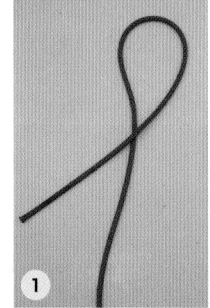

2. Take a bight of the standing end through this bight...

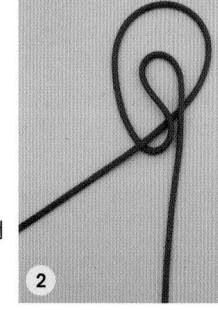

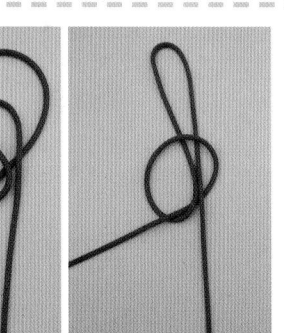

3. And pull tight.

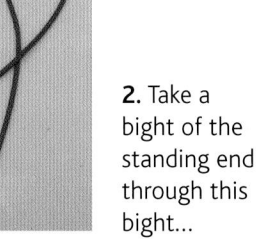

HITCHES

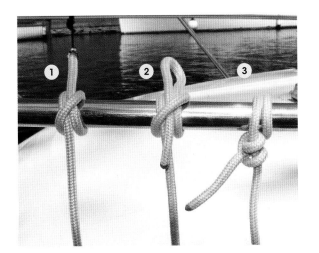

Knots for fenders

1. Clove hitch.

2. Slipped clove hitch.

3. Round turn and two half hitches.

1. Rolling hitch (traditional) *running end crosses over standing part.*

2. Rolling hitch (variant) *running end does not cross over standing part.*

3. Cow hitch.

4. Rustler's hitch (see page 27).

Knots

KNOTS TO SHORTEN ROPE

A bowline in a doubled line.

A bowline on a bight.

An alpine butterfly knot.

An overhand knot.

ON BOARD

Aft Towards the stern
Forward Towards the bow
Beam The widest part of the vessel
Ahead In front of you
Astern Behind you
Gunwale The top of the side of a boat

ANCHORS

Bower anchor Main anchor on the bow
Kedge anchor Spare (secondary) anchor
Windlass Device for lowering and raising the bower anchor – can be manual or electric
Gypsy The keyed wheel that grips the anchor chain/warp

LINE

Bridle A line that connects to the boat at two points
Spring A line that connects to the boat at one point
Slipped line A line running from the boat, round something ashore and back to the boat that can be slipped when you release the running end and haul on the standing end

DRIVES

Shaft drive Inboard engine with propeller on the end of a shaft
Sail drive Inboard engine with propeller on a fixed leg just abaft the keel

Stern drive Inboard engine with the propeller on a steerable leg at the stern
Outboard Outboard steerable engine
Knot 1 nautical mile per hour

ROPE

Warp Rope
Make fast To tie off
Running end The end of the rope you haul on
Working end The end of the rope after the knot, aka the running end
Standing end/part The part of the rope that is made fast – the part of the rope before the knot

ACCESSORIES

Carabiner A clip with a sprung gate
Snap hook A carabiner that allows you to hold the gate open
Snatch block A block that can be opened to feed the rope in rather than having to thread the line through

WIND

Initial The original forecast direction of the wind
Veered The wind direction moves clockwise
Backed The wind direction moves anticlockwise
Windage The amount of superstructure, masts, hull your boat presents that the wind can act upon

Beaufort Force wind speeds		
Force	*Called*	*Knots*
F0	Calm	0–1
F1	Light air	1–3
F2	Light breeze	4–6
F3	Gentle breeze	7–10
F4	Moderate breeze	11–16
F5	Fresh breeze	17–21
F6	Strong breeze	22–27
F7	Near gale	28–33
F8	Gale	34–40
F9	Severe gale	41–47
F10	Storm	48–55
F11	Violent storm	53–63
F12	Hurricane force	>64 There are 5 levels of hurricane force

Glossary

Index